Affinity Publisher
for
Basic Book Covers

AFFINITY PUBLISHER FOR
SELF-PUBLISHING - BOOK 3

M.L. HUMPHREY

SELECT TITLES BY M.L. HUMPHREY

CONTENTS

INTRODUCTION

In *Affinity Publisher for Ad Creatives* we walked through some basic tools that you can use to put together images for Amazon A+ Content, website banners, Facebook ads, BookBub ads, etc.

I want to continue what we started there and now show you how to do some basic ebook covers as well as how to take an existing ebook cover and turn it into a simple paperback or hard cover.

Specifically, we are going to walk through how to:

- Create two ebook covers that use a single image and solid-colored background for the title text

- Create an ebook cover that uses a single image for the entire background

- Create a paperback print cover for use on Amazon using a solid colored background

- Create a paperback print cover for use on IngramSpark using a solid colored background

- Create a case laminate hard cover for use on IngramSpark using a solid colored background

I want to remind you that these books use Affinity Publisher not Affinity Photo.

Even though Publisher isn't the best Affinity program for advanced cover design, it actually works very well for simple design projects like the ones we're going to cover in this book.

And I personally prefer to work in Affinity Publisher because I'm already working with it for my interior book layouts so I don't have to relearn how to perform a task, such as placing an image, that works in a slightly different way in Affinity Photo. (But ultimately if you do want to start combining images and doing more advanced covers, that's where you'll need to go. Plenty of tutorials that work for Photoshop will also work for Affinity Photo.)

Alright. Moving on.

Many of the tools we will use here are the same ones we used for ad creatives, but we're also going to use a few more tools and techniques and broaden our use of the tools you already learned.

(If you didn't read the book on ad creatives, you should still be okay, just know that the books were written to flow from one to the next so I might cover things a little faster this time around, but there's always the Appendix for the thirty-second version of how to do everything I mention in case you feel a little lost.)

Once again, I also want to reiterate that I am not a graphic design professional. No one is going to be paying me $600 for a cover anytime soon. What we are going to create here are *basic* covers. They get the job done, but we're not going to be doing image-blending or mask layers or any of that fun stuff that can really take covers to a different level.

This is just the basics. Taught by a self-published author who doesn't have enough patience to wait six months for a cover or the funds to pay for covers for short stories that may only sell ten copies.

Now, having said that, I do think that the skills you'll learn here are absolutely of value and that I can teach them to you.

So without further ado, let's dive in on some design principles. I'm going to reiterate what we covered in the ad creatives book, but also add some detail around print versus screen colors, element legibility, and fonts.

DESIGN PRINCIPLES

COLOR

RECAP

As a reminder, each genre or category of book has its own color scheme. As a good example, look at the difference between dark romance and sweet romance. Even without the other cover elements involved, you can usually tell a dark romance from a sweet romance on color scheme alone.

Which means the first rule for any cover design is to know where your book fits and to use the colors that apply to books like yours. Keep in mind when doing this research that miscategorizing of books is fairly rampant on Amazon, so you really do need to know who writes what you write.

Colors can also have cultural meanings and feelings associated with them. A bright red is different from a pale yellow in terms of what it conveys to the viewer.

When in doubt, choose complementary colors. These are ones that sit opposite one another on the color wheel.

Contrast is also good. This is why you see so much black on white, white on black in ordinary signage. Because the more contrast there is between text and background the more likely it is someone can read the text.

Okay, now on to the new information with respect to color:

PRINT VS SCREEN COLORS

As a recap, the way that color is created on a computer or phone screen (using light) is different from the way that color is created when it's printed (using ink). For computers, the colors are RGB colors. For print, the colors are CMYK colors.

What this means for you in Affinity is that for print you should set your project up to use CMYK so that you're seeing a more true version of what the project will look like when you actually print. But still, the best thing to do is to actually print out your paperback cover. Do not trust what you see on the screen.

And if you are unsure of your colors, definitely order a proof copy. I once had a cover that looked like it was red on the screen, but it printed bright pink. Which was not good because the target audience was men who would not be drawn to a pink cover.

Personally I've not had issues with blues or blacks, but I have definitely seen variety in bright green and red.

Now, some people will adjust their print covers to make them as close to their ebook covers as possible and you can definitely try to do so. I personally tend to leave my print covers unadjusted and simply accept that my print covers will come out darker.

Because I'm using simple designs, this isn't generally a big issue. If you're using complex images, like in an illustrated cover, it can be a bigger problem because an image that looked fine on the screen can look muddy when printed.

So definitely order a print proof if you get that fancy. (And print it off on your printer first. It's possible you'll see you have issues without having to waste the time and money to get that print proof in the mail.)

Also, keep in mind that even if you adjust your print cover so that it will look good when it prints, the thumbnail version available on vendor websites that readers look at to decide whether or not to buy your book is still going to be displayed electronically using RGB colors.

Okay, now let's talk about element placement and legibility.

ELEMENT PLACEMENT AND LEGIBILITY

RECAP

Remember the rule of thirds as well as the golden ratio.

The rule of thirds is where you split the area you're working with into thirds both horizontally and vertically and try to place key elements of your design either within those sections or at the power points where the lines intersect.

The golden ratio of 1:1.618 can be another design approach to work with either with elements in an image or to determine the relative size of different text elements. So, for example, series name is in X pt size and title is in 1.618 times X pt size.

Also, keep in mind that for most self-published authors, even your print sales will happen online. So subtlety isn't going to help you. Your cover needs to work in thumbnail size on a page with probably a dozen other covers trying to draw your buyer's attention.

ELEMENT LEGIBILITY

Let's expand on that issue of legibility for a minute.

I often see people talk about some really cool thing they're doing with their print cover. Like a really subtle pattern that will look so cool up close. Which could be a nice little bonus for a reader who buys the print book.

But if that cool, subtle pattern makes for a confusing and muddied thumbnail? That's a fail. Because the customer is never going to order the book and see the cool little detail.

(It's like the person who says their book gets really interesting in Chapter 10. If readers put down the book before Chapter 10 because they're bored, that great twist does not matter. It has to draw them in up front and keep them reading until Chapter 10.)

Another issue I've seen is images that are too complicated for a thumbnail view. I think this issue stems from trying to model covers off of trade-published books, which at least historically are much more likely to be bought in a bookstore. As a self-published author, always be looking at your book cover in thumbnail before you finalize it.

It has to work at that tiny size. Print or ebook, it doesn't matter.

If your cover doesn't attract your reader in that little thumbnail size on Amazon, it's not an effective cover.

FONT

RECAP

Your choice of font is incredibly important. As important as any image on your cover. Look at other books in your category to see what kinds of fonts are being used for your type of book.

You don't need to know the entire history of fonts, but do know that there are main categories of font, like serif vs. sans-serif, and that some fonts have a very heavy history that can skew perceptions for those who know that font. Think Comic Sans as a good example.

Once more we have the issue of the thumbnail. But when we're dealing with a cover it's possible that the legibility of the title and author name are secondary to the main image on the cover, especially if that image is a dragon (for fantasy) or a shirtless man (for high-heat romance), for example.

HIERARCHY

Let's expand on the issue of hierarchy when it comes to fonts. Generally, the more important elements on your cover should be in a larger font size than the less important elements.

So your title should be a larger font size than your series name, for example. And your series name should probably be a larger font size than your review quotes, if you have any.

But author name can be tricky. If you're a famous author like Stephen King or Nora Roberts, your name sells your books. And it's the name that matters more than the title or even the cover image.

Sometimes using a larger author name can imply that you're a best-selling author even when you aren't. But I suspect that will change over time as more people try that trick and then readers get savvy to the fact that just because a name on the cover is big it doesn't mean a best-selling or interesting book.

Basically, when determining relative font sizes ask yourself what you want the reader to see first, and make that the largest element, preferably at the top. Although, once more, pay attention to your category or genre because some have very strong trends towards where title and author name are placed.

ALIGNMENT

One final thing to be aware of when dealing with fonts. Each letter in a font is essentially in a small equally-sized rectangle. Different letters will fill that rectangle to different degrees. A lower case letter for example, will not fill that rectangle as much as the same letter in upper case. And the lower-case letter "g" is going to fill that space more than the lower-case letter "e" as another example.

Each word you use is created by combing these rectangles. This becomes an issue when you try to use a program like Affinity to center a line of text. Because Affinity is centering that text based upon the rectangle that contains each letter, not the actual top and bottom of the letters on the page. You can tell Affinity to center that text and it will do so, correctly, using the rectangles, but to the naked eye the text will not be centered.

This is especially an issue with fonts that I think of as "bottom-heavy". These fonts tend to leave more white space above the tops of the letters than below the bottom of the letters.

Which means, depending on the font you choose, you may need to manually center your text in situations like that. (Or choose a better font that doesn't have that issue.)

This is especially important to keep an eye on when looking at the spine of a print book where it becomes very noticeable.

It's also why I often will use all caps on the spine of a book rather than upper- and lower-case letters. That can go a long ways towards alleviating the issue.

Another thing to keep in mind is that some fonts are good at creating ligatures for you and some are not. Due to the nature of certain letters in a font, they can potentially overlap in ugly ways. So "f" and "i" is an example where for some fonts the f curves down enough to almost hit the dot on the i. A good font will swap out the individual letters for a ligature that combines the two in a visually appealing way.

Especially when looking at your title or larger text elements, pay attention to the spacing between individual letters. You may need to manually adjust the space between two letters to make things look "right".

Okay. On to a new topic, series branding.

SERIES BRANDING

If you're creating covers for a related series of books, you want readers to instantly know those books belong together.

This means that you have to make the covers consistent across the collection or series.

A perfect example of this is the J.D. Robb books. She's up to 55 books as I write this and once you get past the first three books, all of the covers share a common appearance. The author name is always in the same place, uses the same font, and takes up about the same amount of space on the cover. Same with title placement and the central cover image.

Here are four of the books in that series:

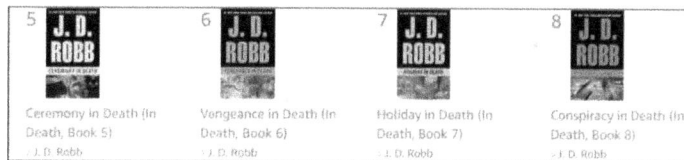

They clearly belong together.

(This is also a perfect example of what I was talking about with big author names, because the first three books did not have the author name dominating the space, but the covers from book four onward do.)

The design is not perfectly aligned across all of those covers, but they still clearly belong together.

And these covers also show that there's plenty of room for variety even within those constraints by changing up the color of the author name, the background color behind the name, and the image used.

When you set out to create the first cover for a series or related collection of titles, you need to think about the entire series and what you can do to have consistent branding across it so that readers immediately know that this is an X series book. This includes thinking through the different titles you might use and making sure that your design can accommodate them.

Also, I want to add here that it is fine to get inspiration from someone else's covers, but do not under any circumstances copy the overall branding of someone else's cover. That is a trademark violation. Even if they don't have that overall look trademarked they can still sue you because trademark is about brand recognition and the fact that someone mistook your book for theirs means you took it too far.

Your cover should never be designed in such a way that it is mistaken for someone else's books. I've seen this only a handful of times in the last eight years because it's almost impossible to copy so many elements from someone else's cover that you get mistaken for their cover. We're not talking common elements, like glowy hands in urban fantasy. This is top to bottom, same element placement, same font, same colors, etc. Do not be that asshole.

* * *

Okay, those are the basics of design. There's far more to it and I would encourage you to research more because it is so important to selling books, but this is not a book about design principles, this is a book about putting your design elements together to make book covers.

So let's move on and do that.

I'm going to assume your workspace is already organized like mine from the ads creative book, but if it isn't at a minimum make sure that your Layers studio is in the top right corner and your Transform studio is in the bottom right corner.

EBOOK COVER WITH A CENTRAL IMAGE

Okay. Let's start with an easy one, and that's an ebook cover that uses a single image and solid-colored block for the text like we just saw with the J.D. Robb covers.

There can be a lot of variety in taking this approach. Here are two different covers I've designed over the years that use a central image.

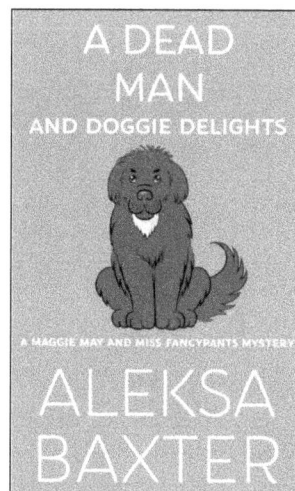

They're great for short story collections or long series that need uniformity across books.

For example, here are the first four books in the Puppy Love series:

They clearly fit together, right? And all I had to do was change out the photo, change the number for the book in the series, and change the title. Everything else stays the same for each story.

Which means that once the template is in place it only takes about five minutes to create each new cover. Maybe ten. The hardest part is finding a good image to use.

That and dealing with any issues if the title for a particular book or story is significantly different and messes up the design. But that's why you try not to have titles that are vastly different across a series.

The other option is to use a layout like I did with the M.H. Lee titles that uses a design that allows for vastly different title lengths but still keeps that uniformity of appearance:

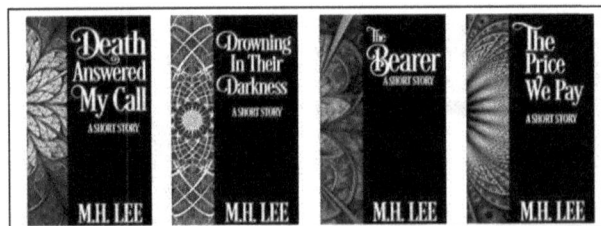

(Those might've taken a little longer than five minutes each because of the font I chose for the cover which required some playing around each time.)

Alright then. For this first cover, we're going to create a new Puppy Love cover from scratch.

I'm going to assume you know how to create a new document and, if wanted, a preset, and that your workspace is set up for working with images. That was all covered in *Affinity Publisher for Ad Creatives*, but see the Appendix for the short version of how to do each if you don't remember or didn't read that book first.

Step one is to start with a new document that fits ebook cover dimensions. Mine are currently set to 1600 x 2560. I used to use 1563 x 2501.

(Don't ask me why I changed. I think the first set of dimensions I used came straight from Amazon's help text somewhere, but the second set made Vellum happier, but don't quote me on that. Both of those dimensions work fine on all retailers as far as I've seen.)

So, File->New, enter the dimensions or use your preset, RGB/8 is fine for the color, and profile for the orientation.

As for DPI…I personally use 300 DPI for any cover I'm creating even ebook, because this lets me bring that ebook cover image into my print layouts without worrying about the image being blurry when printed.

The minimum DPI you want for print is 300 and the only way to effectively get that throughout your design process is to start with it. (We'll discuss the mistakes I've made in this regard more when we talk about creating a print cover.)

The reason not to use 300 DPI for an ebook cover is potential file size. But you can fix some of that with your export settings.

So I'm going with 300 DPI. You should at least use a minimum of 72 DPI.

Once you have your settings, click Create and you will have a nice white space to work with.

Before we do anything else, let's place guide lines to divide our space into thirds. I'm working with 1600 x 2560 so that means 533 and 1066 for my vertical lines and 853 and 1707 for my horizontal lines.

You can place guide lines by left-clicking on the ruler along the left-hand edge or the top of the workspace and then dragging them into place. You will see a small box appear with the position of the guideline as you drag it into place.

Stop when you reach the location you want. Left-click on the line and drag again to adjust if you get it wrong the first time. That will leave you with something like this where the blue lines are my guide lines that are dividing my cover into nine sections.

(To avoid having to do this every single time you create a cover, you may want to save this blank cover with guide lines as its own file that you can start with next time you want to create a cover.)

For the Puppy Love covers, I devoted the top third to the title and series information so our next step is to place a solid fill for the top third and a picture frame for the bottom two-thirds.

To do this, click on the Rectangle Tool on the left-hand side and click and drag in the workspace to create a solid-colored rectangle in the top third of the cover. Then click on the Picture Frame Rectangle Tool on the left-hand side and click and drag to form the picture frame in the bottom two-thirds of the cover.

Remember that you want Snapping Enabled (top menu with the horseshoe shaped magnet, in the dropdown click on the checkbox to Enable Snapping) so that when you drag your elements into place you can see the red and green lines that show that they are aligned with your other elements, the perimeter of the cover, and/or the guide lines you placed.

In the image above there is a red line across the canvas at the one-third mark where we placed a guide line and also there's one through the center of the picture frame to show that it's centered in the space. We could click and drag out and then back on any of the perimeter lines to see that the frame is aligned with the edges of the workspace as well. (I already did that as I clicked and dragged to place the frame.)

Next, we want to change the color of the Rectangle we placed, so click on the rectangle layer in the Layers studio:

We now have a few choices for changing the color of the rectangle. We can go to the dynamic menu at the top which has a rounded rectangle next to the word Fill, click on that, and choose a color from there:

Or, we can click on the Color studio, double-click on the solid-filled circle which shows our current color, and then use the Color Chooser to find or specify our color.

As you can see in the image above, there are a number of different approaches to choose from in the dropdown provided for the Color Chooser.

If I'm just moving between basic colors like black and white or I'm using a color I've already used in my design, I go with the Fill option at the top of the workspace. But if I have a specific color I want to use or want to really experiment with choosing a new color, I use the Color studio.

So let's go with the Color studio right now. I'm going to choose the HSL Color Wheel option. And I want some sort of bright pink.

These are ebook-only covers so I don't need to worry about how the color will print which means I can do something bright and not worry too much about how dark it will be when printed.

I like that color on my high resolution monitor. It looks nice and bright pink. But interestingly enough—and I can't show you this, unfortunately—when I look at the screenshot of this on my laptop I see a more muted, almost purple color.

And I think this is important to understand. That not all of your viewers are going to experience whatever it is you create in the same way. It will depend very much on the device they are using to view your cover. I've also seen this difference when I move from my PC laptop where I design my covers to my Apple laptop where I generate my Vellum ebook files.

But I know right now, just looking between my laptop and my monitor, that some users are going to see a bright pink background on this cover and others are going to see a more muted purple.

If it's really important to me that everyone see pink, then I need to click further along on the color wheel towards red.

I now have a very vibrant pink on my monitor and a more muted pink on my laptop screen, but at least they're both pink, so we'll go with it.

While I'm here, I may want to write down my HSL values for this color, in this case 310, 100, and 50. Because for the heart I'm going to put on this section to show which number in the series a title is, I want a color that's as vibrant as the one I'm using for the background.

Since my S value is 100 I probably don't need to do this, but when you get away from the color extremes—so the colors in the triangle rather than around the perimeter—it can matter more if you want the colors to feel like they belong together.

By keeping my S at 100 and my L at 50 I can change the H value to get bright blues, greens, yellows, etc. that all feel like they go with my pink.

One more thing to mention before we move on from the color wheel. For a series if you do want to use different colors consider dividing the color wheel into sections and then changing the H value by the same amount for each new cover.

So I might go from 310 for this pink to 250, which gives me a bright blue, to 190 which is a lighter blue, to 120 which is a bright green, to 60 which is a bright yellow. It's possible not all of the colors will be ones you want to use—I'd probably skip the light blue—but doing that can give you a range of colors to play with that also seem to fit together well as opposed to being more random about it.

Okay.

Time to add text. I don't think I did this with the original covers, but I'm going to use a text frame here so that the text stays in the same space even when we change up the title. So let's click on the Frame Text Tool (the T in a gray box) and then draw a frame for our title text.

Ideally you never want to take any of your key image elements to the edge of the cover. It should have a little room to breathe. (I am admittedly bad at remembering this.)

And looking at this space I don't think trying to contain either the series name or the title to one-third of the space we're working with is going to look good, but maybe what I can do is use that golden ratio and make my text frame fit a 1 to 1.6 ratio.

It's not going to be visible to the viewer that I've done that, because my text won't ever fill the entire space, but it might help to block out that space.

So my top text frame is going to be 788 W by 493 H. And then I'm going to draw a second text frame below that that's the same width, but only 110 H. (I may adjust that later.)

Let's put some text in each of those boxes.

I'll start with the author name, in this case "C. Coal". To do so, I make sure I'm clicked onto that layer in my Layers studio, click on the A for the Artistic Text Tool, and then click into that text frame in my workspace and type in the name.

I now have the top left corner of that text frame showing C. Coal in black, Arial, 12 pt because that's the default.

I select all (Ctrl +A) and then click on the black rectangle in the dynamic menu up top and change my color to white. I was able to just double-click on the white full circle in the dropdown but if that wasn't white I could've gone to the Swatches tab and clicked on the white swatch there.

I also changed my font size to 24 pt.

I want left-aligned, so that's fine, but I'm going to go into the alignment dropdown and center that text vertically as well as you can see in the screenshot below.

Most designers would probably say that Arial is a boring font you should never use for a cover design. Just like using Times New Roman on a cover. Which, fine, whatever. It doesn't really have a personality so I can see that, but I don't find it objectionable to use it either. If what you want is something that is innocuous and conveys information without interference, I think it works well for that.

But let's go hunting for a better font to use.

To do that, click on the dropdown for the font in the top menu. (Or in the Character studio if you'd rather use that). And you should see a listing of available fonts like this:

I have a lot of fonts. (DesignCuts and their bundles have been my downfall.)

And because with cover design you need to be careful that you have a commercial license for the font you use, I actually went through one day and created for myself a PDF that shows each of the fonts I have a license to use.

(Because the ones that are there as part of Microsoft Office, for example, are not necessarily available for your commercial use in your cover design even though Affinity might pull them up for you.)

It's an Excel file which means if I know I want a specific type of font, like serif or sans-serif, I can filter the file to just that type of font. But I also have it in PDF so I can scan through visually, too.

I put the word "Handgloves" in front of each of the fonts so I could see how it treated that word, which is supposed to be a good word to use to see how a font handles ascenders and descenders. (That's the d and l and the g.)

Also, I have a personal issue with how some fonts handle a "g", especially script fonts, so writing Handgloves let me see that easily.

Here's the first page of the PDF:

Sample (20 pt)	Style	Font Name
HANDGLOVES ARISTELLE SANS	Display	Handgloves Aristelle Sans
Handgloves Bauhaus 93	Display	Handgloves Bauhaus 93
HANDGLOVES BEACHWOOD SANS	Display	Handgloves Beachwood Sans
Handgloves	Display	Handgloves Betterworks
Handgloves BlackChancery	Display	Handgloves BlackChancery
Handgloves Boyz R Gross	Display	Handgloves Boyz R Gross
Handgloves Bradley Gratis	Display	Handgloves Bradley Gratis
Handgloves Bradley Hand ITC	Display	Handgloves Bradley Hand ITC
Handgloves Brittanic Bold	Display	Handgloves Brittanic Bold
Handgloves Broadway	Display	Handgloves Broadway
HANDGLOVES BRUNCHES	Display	Handgloves Brunches
HANDGLOVES BRUSHABS	Display	Handgloves Brushabs
HANDGLOVES BUSHCRAFT SANS	Display	Handgloves Bushcraft Sans
HANDGLOVES CARENTRO	Display	Handgloves Carentro
Handgloves Carolingua (Bigfoot)	Display	Handgloves Carolingua (Bigfoot)

Ignore the "Handgloves" part of the font name in the third column. That was just my weirdness putting it in there and I've been too lazy to have Excel strip it back out for me.

(Looking at this you can also see how different fonts have vastly different heights at the same point size. Look at Betterworks compared to Beachwood Sans. These are all in 20 pt font.)

For this cover I want something fairly simple and maybe a little fun. Which means Brunches might be a good option for the title and author name.

I have it listed as a display font, but it's also sans-serif which is what I want. (For my listing if I think a font could be main body text for the interior that's what I show as a serif or sans-serif, but if I think it would work on a cover but not in the main body of a document I show it as display even if it is also serif or sans-serif. I like to be confusing, but it works for me.)

So looking at these fonts…

Something like Beachwood Sans or Bauhaus have too much personality for what I want here. The series name portion is going to be in a script font, so I want a font for the title and author name that doesn't fight with that.

I can go back into Affinity and actually try these out in real-time. As I slowly move my mouse over each font in the dropdown menu, Affinity will change my text on the canvas to that font. Like here where it's applied the Brunches font to my author name:

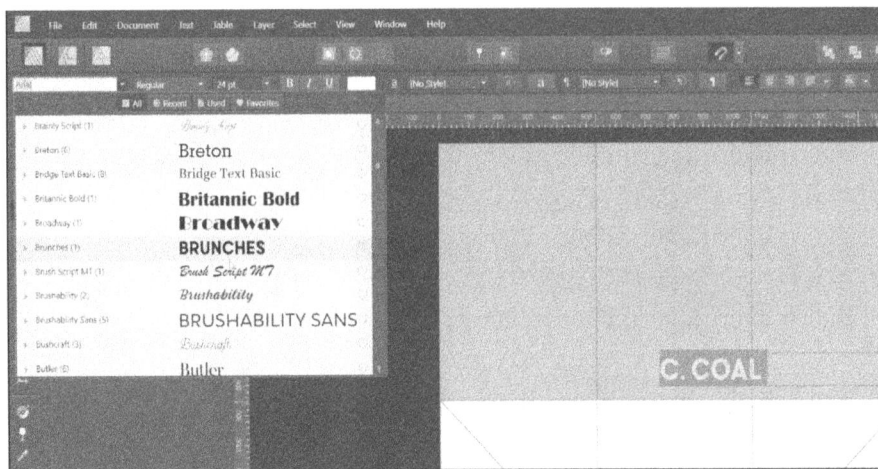

It's just doing this temporarily. I'd have to actually click on the font name for Affinity to permanently apply it to the text. But scrolling down is a quick way to see which fonts may or may not work in the design. (Just always be sure to check that you have the license for the font before you finalize your design.)

If I think a font might work, I'll usually save or export a draft version of the cover with that font applied and then keep looking for other options.

I want to say with the original of this cover I came up with twenty-five different possibilities.

Once I have those possible covers exported to a file I can then go to the folder where I saved them and start doing a side-by-side elimination. I look at Cover 1 and Cover 2 and decide that 1 is better so delete 2. And then that 3 is better than 1 and so delete 1. And so on and so on until I get down to about five covers that are all equally fine

And then I pick one out of the remaining group.

Here I think Brunches was a little chunky for what I wanted. Brushability Sans was a little thin. It turns out in this case that I used a font called Explorer Sans and I used the bold version. This font does come in smaller than other fonts at this point size so I also needed to increase the font size to use it.

A quick note here. I've been talking about fonts but I also tend to use the term font for font family, which is a technical no-no. So let me break that down real quick.

Explorer Sans Regular is a font. Explorer Sans Bold is technically a *different* font because it's a different weight. Both would be considered part of the same font family because they have the same general appearance and design.

Where it gets confusing is that I also have an Explorer P Sans and an Explorer Script option which are probably technically considered part of the Explorer font family, but one has a rough surface appearance and the other is a script font.

So I just in my sloppy way refer to fonts which can either be the individual font, Explorer Sans Bold, or can be the entire family. Keep that in mind for the next little bit.

Okay.

If you don't have various weights/styles of a font, they won't be options for you to choose from in Affinity. Like here, the font I have right above Explorer Sans is called Euphoria Script, but I only have one weight of that font so my dropdown for weight for that font only lists Regular as an option:

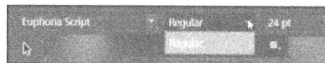

I also can't do italics for that font. It is what it is.

Compare that to Kenac where I have ten options available, five different weights, all with an italic ("It") version:

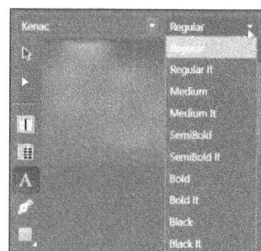

With this one I can keep the appearance of the Kenac font, but have various versions of it on my cover that are thinner or thicker or slanted.

Always keep that in mind when selecting the fonts you're going to use on your cover.

If you're going to have a lot of text elements like title, author name, series name, and review quote, for example, you may want to choose a font family that has multiple weights and italic versions to give you some variety in your design.

What you do not want to do is use more than two font families—including any display fonts—in your design. And only use one serif font family and one sans serif font family at a time. Do not have your two font families be two serif families or two sans serif families.

Each font family you choose needs to be different enough to hold its own.

Okays. So Explorer Sans. And I'm going to make it 36 pt.

This brings up an interesting issue I mentioned to you before, and that's fonts that are bottom-heavy or that basically don't fit evenly in their text frame. Because look at this:

I have that text centered vertically. It should be sitting in the center of the text frame with equal amounts of space above and below the letters. But it is not. And if I align it to the top it doesn't go to the top. Align it to the bottom and it's fine, but there's extra space built in above the letters of this font.

So if I were to use this right now and have Affinity center that text top to bottom on my page the text would not in fact be centered. The space the text is in would, but not the actual letters, which is what really matters.

So be careful when choosing your font that you pay attention to something like this and realize the issues it's going to cause you. Here it doesn't cause me any issue, but if I were to do a print version of this cover and use the same font on the spine, it definitely would.

Okay.

Let me add a title for this one into the text frame above. I'm going to call this one Spring Fling. So I click on the A for the Artistic Text Tool, click into the other text frame, and type in my text. And then I have to change my font, font size, color, and weight.

Looking at it, I think that I actually want the font size to go up to 48 instead of 36, so now I do that for both text frames.

But we run into an issue. The text frame I have for the author name isn't large enough to display 48 pt text in this font. Affinity indicates that by not displaying the text on my canvas, but instead showing red circles along the perimeter of the text frame. There's also an alert in the Preflight studio.

I can still see the text in the Layers studio however.

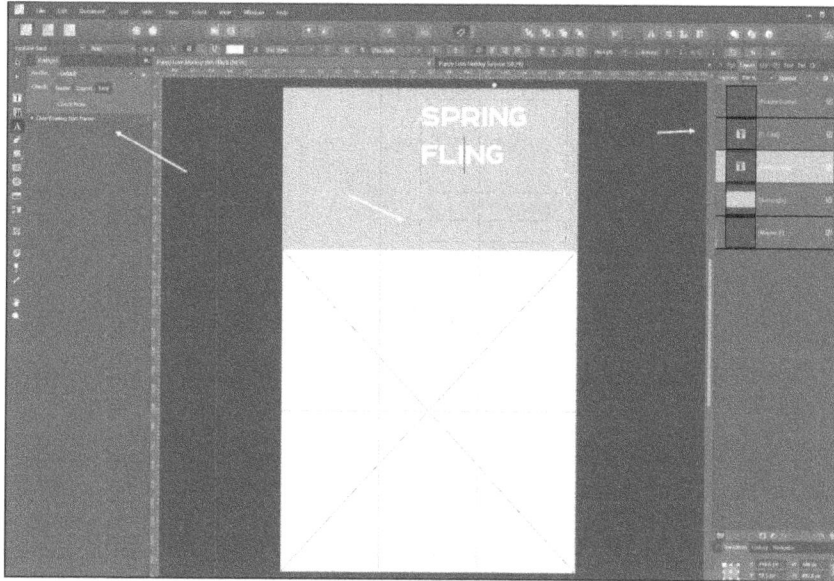

I have two choices. Change the font size back or change the size of the text frame.

I am going to change the size of the text frame. To do so I click on the frame in the Layers studio, click on the blue circle at the top of the frame in my workspace, and drag until my text becomes visible again. Since the text frame for my author name and for my title still don't overlap, that's all I have to do.

But we have another issue to deal with now. I don't like the spacing between the lines in my title section:

I think those lines are too far apart.

There are two choices you have here to fix this.

You can use separate text frames for each line of text and manually space them until you get an appearance you like. This is often the answer when you have words like "the" and "to" that are small and you have to include them because they're part of the title, but don't want them to be as large as the rest of your text.

Or you can leave the text together and go to the Character studio and change the line spacing, otherwise known as Leading.

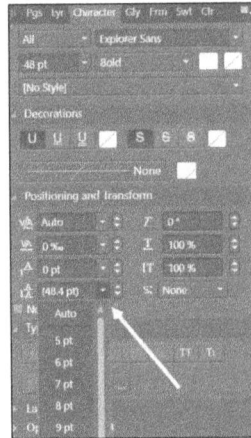

To do that, select your text and then go to the Character studio and click on the dropdown arrow for leading override. Hold your mouse over each option to see what it will look like on the canvas until you get one that works.

In this case I decided that 30 is a little too tight and 36 is a little too loose, so I typed in 32. That works for me.

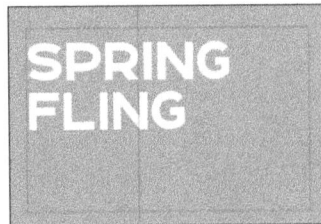

(And another note here that design is subjective. There are probably some who'd feel those letters are crowding each other a little too much and would go with the 36 pt setting. And maybe tomorrow I would, too. That's why it's good to try to let a design sit a bit if you can so you can come back to it after a few days and think, "Yeah, no, that doesn't work" or "Okay, yeah, we're good." Especially as a novice designer. Professionals have things they know work from hundreds of hours of experience. As a novice you have to build that experience. Until you do, expect to make mistakes.)

Okay. Our title and our author name are there. Let's do the easy part and throw in a picture of a cute puppy. So click on the Layers studio, click on the Picture Frame layer, go to the tools on the left-hand side, click on the Place Image Tool, find your image, and open it.

How about a cute bulldog:

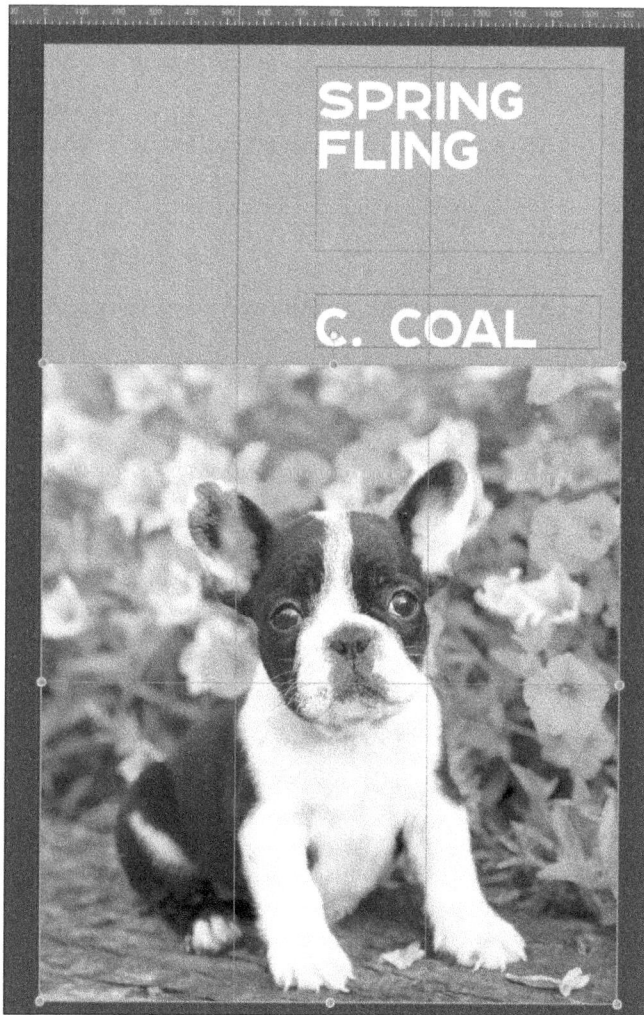

That's how the image came in. He's actually pretty well positioned according to the guide lines, but I think I want to make him a little bigger. I also don't like the pink of the flowers behind him compared to the pink in the background up top. That background pink is back to looking to purple for me.

Since this is a series cover, assuming it wasn't the first one, I wouldn't be able to change that background color. So if that clash were enough of a problem for me I'd have to choose a different image because I'm not advanced enough (or interested enough) in changing the color of the flowers in the image.

But since this is the first cover we've done for this series, we can change that background color.

First, I'm going to increase the size of the image and reposition it. I can either use the slider below the image to change its size and click in the center of the four arrows on the image to reposition it, or I can click on the picture frame layer, click down to the image, and resize and move from there.

Now for the color. I go to the Color studio and use the eyedropper tool to grab a pink from the flowers behind the dog. Remember, left-click on the eyedropper and hold as you hover over the canvas. Let up when you find a color you like. Double-click on the circle next to the eyedropper to actually apply it:

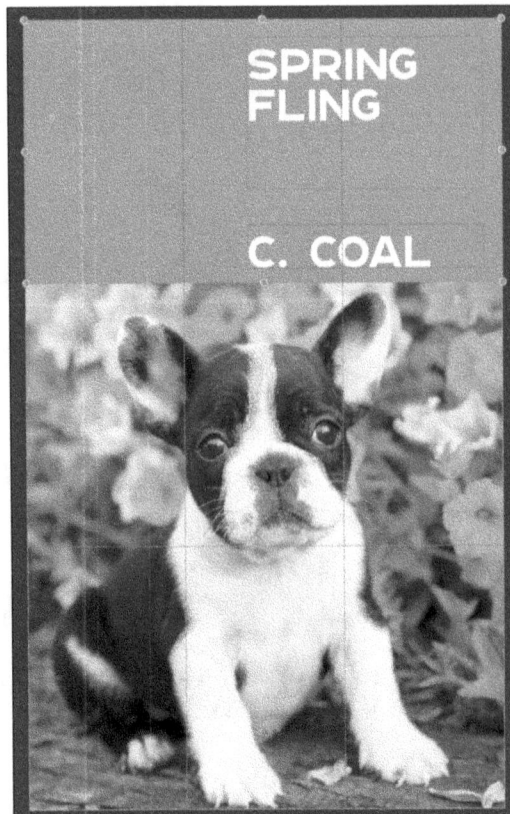

Much better.

That's actually much more pink than the background on the cover was before. Also, increasing the size of the image and bringing that dog into the center rectangle in our rule of thirds really makes his cute little face the focus.

Which is good, because this series of stories is basically for people who love puppies and want to read about them bringing two people together for a stress-free happily ever after. The dog is what is meant to sell the story.

Okay. Now we need to add the series name on the left-hand side and the series number. Since this one isn't going to be changed from cover to cover we can type the text directly onto our cover. So I click on the Artistic Text tool, click on my cover, and type in Puppy, enter, Love.

You'll notice as you work with fonts that sometimes the spacing between lines will be different depending on whether the text wraps to the next line or you use an enter to get text to the next line. All I'd say for that is to choose one or the other to keep it consistent.

Or, as I mentioned above, separate each line of text into its own layer.

Once more we need to change the color, size, font, and line spacing.

Since I used Explorer Sans for the title and author name I'm going to use Explorer Script for the series name. The two fonts are meant to work together and if you have font combinations like that it can sometimes be a good way to have that variety of fonts on your cover but also know that they are made to be paired with one another.

Now it's time to angle our text. There are two options here. You can left-click on the white circle above the text box and drag until the text is at an angle you like.

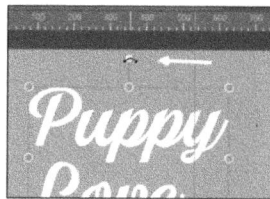

Or you can enter a new R value in the Transform studio. For the original covers I used 15 degrees, but I like 20 degrees better this time around.

Once I have the angle set and the size set I can drag that text into place. I added an extra guide line so that I could align the top of the Puppy text with the top of the title. I also adjusted the font size so that the bottom of my series name lines up with the bottom of the rectangle I created for the title text to fit in.

We'll see if we keep it that way, but here it is:

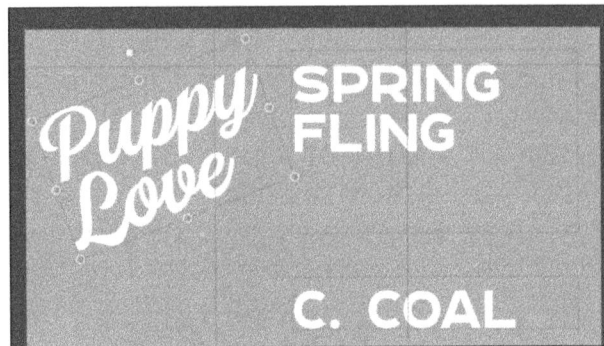

Now all we need is the heart with the number on it to tell us which book this is in the series.

To add a heart shape, go to the Rectangle Tool, click on the white dropdown arrow, and choose the Heart Tool. Then click and drag a heart on the cover just like you would a rectangle.

First things first, let us change the color of that heart.

I want to do this in the Color studio, so go there, and double-click on the pink that's the current color to bring up the Color Chooser dialogue box. Mine is still on the HSL Color Wheel screen since that's what I used last.

(My S and L values are different from what I wrote down above because we changed our pink.)

I want blue but I'm going to keep S as 91 and L as 56. I can just click over along the perimeter of the wheel to get that. And, perfect.

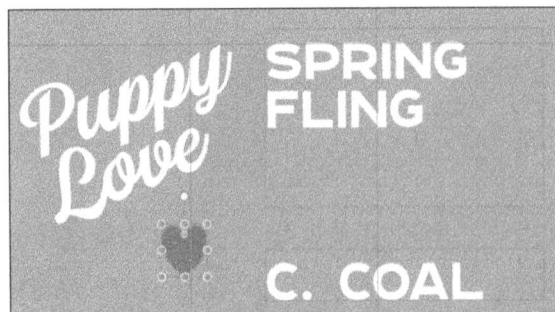

But I want my heart angled like my series title, so I'm going to change that R value to a 20 in the Transform studio.

Note that the Transform studio (and other bottom-level studios) can move around a bit dependent upon which top-level studio you have open. I tend to think it's disappeared on me when it's really just moved up to the midpoint because I have a studio open that doesn't require as much space and have no studios anchored in the middle.

Okay. I can now drag the blue heart into position and adjust its size until I like how it fits with the other elements. In this case I do so until it lines up with the bottom of the word Love and also along the first-third dividing line.

Now I need to add a number on top of that. Click away from the heart, click on A for Artistic Text Tool, click back on the canvas, add the number, change the font, color, etc., change the angle, resize. Click on the Move Tool black arrow and then click and drag the number on top of the heart.

If the number disappears when you do this (as it just did to me) then the number layer is below the heart layer in the Layers studio, and you need to go to the Layers studio and click and drag it up.

If it's still not positioned perfectly, you can use the up and down and right and left arrows to adjust its position on the canvas.

If you decide you want to resize the heart at this point, I'd recommend grouping the heart and number layers so you can resize them together. (Select both and use Ctrl + G to group them.)

Here's the result:

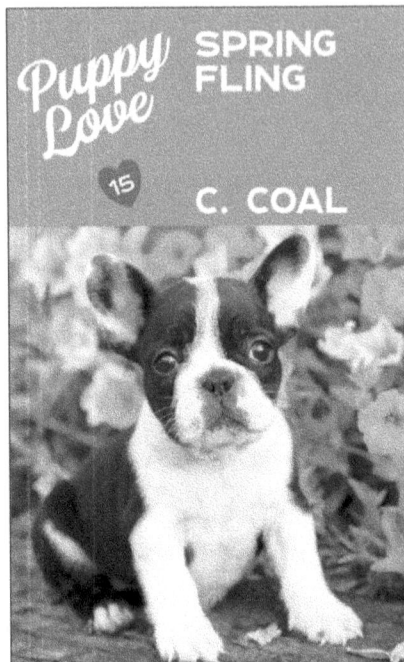

If this was a new cover design I might tweak this a bit more (there's a lot of space there between the title and the author name and I think I'd move the heart around a bit more), but overall I think it does what it needs to do, which is draws the eye to a cute puppy and implies that it's a sweet romance.

You can use this basic design for other genres, though. Just for kicks, let me change this up a smidge to show you.

An image, series name, and some color changes and here we have a sexy romance instead of a clean and sweet one:

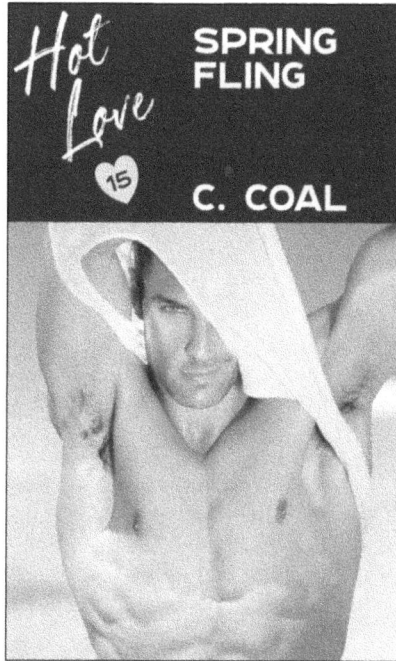

That took about five minutes for me, if that. Granted, the colors here are more for a fun summer fling series than say, a broody bad boy series. But you get the idea that you can use a template like this and then change up the feel of the cover with the image you choose, the font you use, and the colors.

Both of these rely heavily on the image to bring in the reader. One says, "cute puppies." The other says, "hot dude taking off his shirt." For their respective audiences, that draws the eye.

Okay. Now let's take a quick look at an ebook cover that uses a side image instead and leaves two-thirds of the space for the title information. This one we're going to put a lot more attention on font elements because that's what dominates the space.

EBOOK COVER WITH A SIDE IMAGE

Now we're going to build another basic ebook cover that uses a single image and a solid-colored background for the text, but this time the image will be just one-third of the cover and most of the focus is going to be on the title information.

First we need our ebook cover. I saved a version of a blank ebook cover with guide lines on it, so to open that I go to File->Open Recent and choose that file from the dropdown menu. If it wasn't one I'd used recently, I'd do File->Open and navigate to where I had it saved.

This one we're going to put the image for each cover on the left-hand third of the canvas. I'd say this is very much a short story or non-fiction style.

So, Picture Frame Rectangle tool, click and drag to fill the left-hand third of the cover space from top to bottom using the green and red alignment lines to make sure we've hit the edge.

Keep in mind that sometimes it's easier to click and drag onto the canvas and then move each line around the perimeter into position along the edges.

Next, Rectangle Tool. In my case, because the last time I used the "shape tool" it was a heart, I'm currently seeing a blue heart in my left-hand set of icons. But I can click on that white arrow next to the heart, choose the Rectangle Tool, and draw my rectangle in the other two-thirds of the cover.

Mine came in as light gray, so I click on the Fill box in the dynamic menu up top and I turn it black using the Swatches tab:

Very boring. But let's add our image.

Click on the Picture Frame layer in the Layers studio and then use the Place Image Tool to find an image to place on that left-hand third.

I used this design for my speculative fiction covers which are often "an interesting but abstract idea" so that's what I'm going to use for the cover image. Basically I just want something that's different for each one and, honestly with these, I expect the collection to sell not the individual short stories. The individual short stories exist more for me to offer one up for free to drive interest to the collection.

I will also say with both the prior short story series and this one, I don't see many sales of either one. The only short story series I've ever seen good sales on were billionaire romance or erotica. But maybe you will do better. Or you can use a short story as a lead magnet into your series. (Although, as a novel reader the short stories my authors write tend not to do much for me, but that's probably just me.)

Anyway. I'm getting away from what we're doing. So, let's add the image.

But first, let me just take a moment here to talk about stock photos. My advice to you is going to be (a) pay for them and (b) make sure you read the license for the photos you use.

I get my photos from Shutterstock, Depositphotos, and DesignCuts. All of those allow me to use their images in book covers. There was some other site that had an AppSumo deal a few years back where I had to cancel the deal because when I read the terms it didn't seem like I'd be able to use those images the way I needed to.

Also, at least when I first started using them, I noticed that Depositphotos had a time cap on downloaded images. I was buying monthly download packs at the time and it basically said I had to use those downloaded photos within X days. Shutterstock did not.

I now buy the AppSumo Depositphotos deal when it's offered each year around November and that gives me download credits I can then use when I need an image, so that I'm always within that use period.

Can you stretch things? Sure, probably. Do you want to take that risk? Eh...It can be expensive if you get caught out. So always know where you got an image from and what the rights you have to use it are.

The reason I avoid the free sites is because there have been times someone loaded images to one of those sites that were not theirs and then you can get sued for a nice chunk of change if you use that image.

Also, it should be obvious, but just because an image is on the internet does not make it available for you to use. It is copyrighted just like everything you write is copyrighted. So if you don't want people stealing your shit, don't steal theirs.

Okay then. We now have a cover that has an image on the left-hand side and a black spacc to work in on the right two thirds of the cover.

Time to put in our text. I'm going to use one of my obnoxiously-long titles so we have a lot to work with: By Your Side When the Sun Sets by M.H. Lee.

(The real cover for this one has a dragon image in that left-hand third, but right now I'm just using a galaxy background.)

I'm going to use a font I purchased, Desire, for the title and author name because I want you to see how to use the Glyph Browser.

The first thing we need to do before we type in our text is ask, how are we going to split that up? It's messy, right? Where's the emphasis in that title? On Your? Or By? Or Side? Or Sun Sets?

We don't have to stick to this; we can change our minds later. But for now…

I think I'll split it into thirds with "By Your Side", "When", and "the Sun Sets" as my three lines of text. But I'm going to put "the" and "Sun Sets" as separate layers because I want to keep "the" small.

So let's do that.

Choose the Artistic Text Tool and create layers for each of those.

Because it's a black background I need to change the text to white so I can see it. I'm also going to change my font over before I start typing since I have four layers to create and that means less work for me.

You don't have to worry about size right now, but you can.

With the Artistic Text Tool you can actually left-click and drag to form an A (that is not going to be there once you start to type) if you're not sure what font size you need. Just drag to about the desired height for your letters and then type.

Another thing you can do is get all four layers entered and then select all of the layers in the Layers studio. That will put a box around all four of them that you can then click and drag from the corner to change the size of them all at once.

So I input my text and here we are:

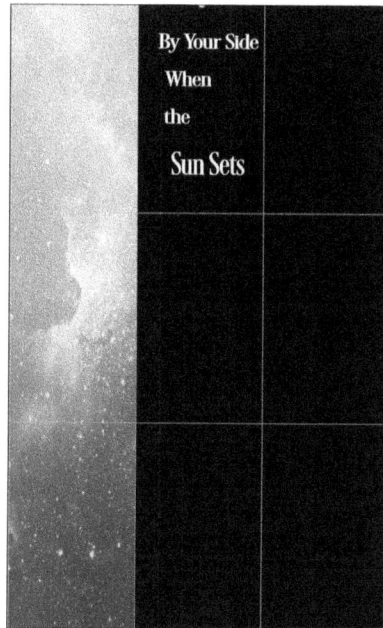

Obviously we're not going to leave it this way. That does not look good. But the first step is always getting the components in place.

Now we need to make some decisions. The first one is where we want to place the title.

I'm thinking the top third. If we place it in the middle third that leaves a lot of dead space up top that won't get used. But if we put the title in the top third of the cover that will leave the middle for any subtitle information and the bottom for the author name.

I'd only put author name at the top if it was a recognizable name that could sell the book on name alone like Stephen King or Nora Roberts. But for us mere mortals, better to put title up top, author down below.

Okay, so that's decided.

Next we get to play around with how to arrange these words. And, really, that comes down to genre and personal preference and design skill. (I can bet money at least one person reading this book can arrange these words better than I'm about to. And to that person I apologize for the painful experience of watching me get it wrong.)

Word placement also depends a lot on the font you're using and the actual words in the title.

Let me show you what I mean. The first word in this title is "By" which means we can maybe do something interesting with that capital B.

Let's go to the Glyph Browser studio and see what our options are:

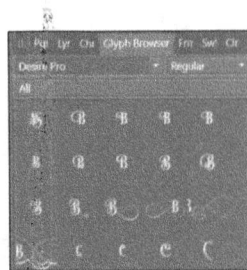

Not bad. I have fifteen variants on a capital B to choose from in this font. (But not the twenty-seven I'd have for a capital A)

What about an S or a T. Let's look at that next:

A decent number of choices. W has about the same.

I also have lower-case letters to potentially play with. And, again, some letters will have more choices than others.

And keep in mind that most fonts will not have this much variety. My first YA fantasy covers used a font called Jupiter which has a couple of alternates for letters like R—there are two fancy ones to choose here—but not near the insane variety that Desire does.

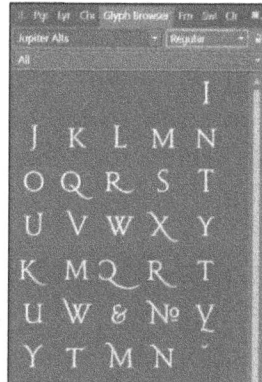

And it also has some ligatures, like these:

So there are some choices that can be made to spice up the text design, but it very much depends on the font and it depends on the letters in the words in the title.

I show you all of this because when I was first looking at covers and thinking, "Wow, that's fancy" I assumed that the cover designer had added all of the flourishes or extensions to the title themselves.

I thought all those whirls and swirls were part of the design work they did. But the reality is that in a lot of instances they just know the right font to use and how to choose the alternates.

Now, neither one of the fonts I just showed you is free. I bought Jupiter because I wanted to be able to match the font used on the covers for my YA fantasy series. And I bought Desire, because, wow, look at all those choices.

(I only learned about Desire, though, after someone I know who is good at covers looked at a mockup a designer had done for a cover for me and said, "Oh,

I think that's using that Desire font that everyone seems to be using these days." So be careful jumping on that particular bandwagon.)

Anyway. Back to our cover and our text.

There are an infinite number of options for how to combine the seven words in this title. And it's very easy to take a font like Desire and get out of control with it. Allow me to demonstrate:

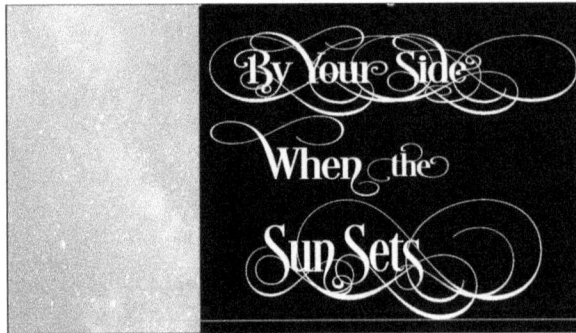

This is just too much. In thumbnail all you see are a bunch of swirls everywhere. Kudos to the font that it doesn't look even worse, but it's bad. People can and do have different aesthetics—I mean some people like toilets made of gold, right—but I'm willing to go out on a limb here and assume that at least nine out of ten people would find this overdone.

So flourishes are nice, but not on every single letter. And certainly not for mainstream science fiction and fantasy.

Okay. Let's do a quick review on how to apply one of these and then we'll try some more reasonable designs.

If the letter is already in the workspace (like here) and you want to replace it, highlight the letter, then go to the Glyph Browser studio, pull up your font, find the version you want to use to replace that letter, and double-click on it.

Remember that you can start to type in the font name in the top menu to find the font and its options faster. Or just scroll through the dropdown menu until you find the font you want.

If there is no letter to replace, just click into your workspace where you want to insert the letter and then go to the Glyph Browser studio and double-click on the option you want.

Recently-used glyphs will be at the bottom of the studio so that you can just double-click on them from there instead of having to look them up.

So let's see what we can do with this text.

First things first, I'm going to move "the" so that it's on the same line with

"Sun Sets". If you have snapping enabled (which you should), you can see when two layers are aligned as you drag them together. Like here where the red line indicates that they're aligned along the bottom of the two text layers:

I can also align vertically. In that case, it's a green line that shows.

I'm going to see what happens when I align the "By", "When" and "the" on the left-hand side.

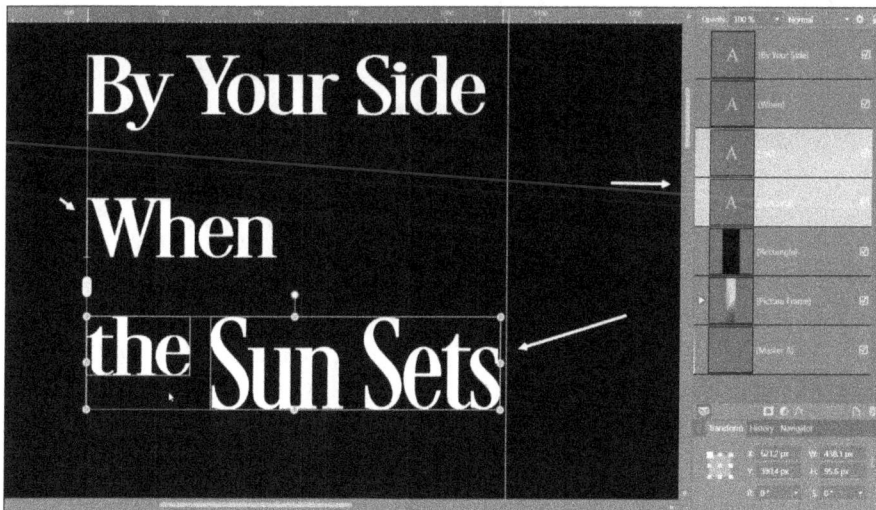

If you want to move two text layers at once, select both of their layers first in the Layers studio by clicking on one and then holding down the Ctrl key or Shift key to select the other. Ctrl if they're not adjacent, Shift or Ctrl if they are.

I've zoomed in here (View->Zoom and then pick an option, I chose 200%) to make it easier to see my text. Usually I don't do this because I like to also see how the elements I'm working on fit in the overall design. (And you'll see in a minute that this created a problem for me.)

Now it's time to make this interesting in some way.

We could just align the text and change some font sizes around and leave it plain. Here I've taken the size of "Sun Sets" which is 32.8 pt and divided that by 1.6 to get 20.5 pt for "the" and then applied those two font sizes to "By Your Side" and "When".

I wanted to keep the three lines of text evenly spaced. I could have done it manually by selecting each line and moving it up and down and watching the numbers that appear between the layers until they matched.

But what I did instead is group the "the" and "Sun Sets" layers into one layer and then group all three text lines into another layer. I then selected those three layers and went to the Alignment option up top and chose the Space Vertically option under the Align Vertically section.

This option isn't working for me, though. "When" is too prominent.

So let's change that up and make "By" smaller so I can make "Your Side" bigger to better match the "When".

I'm also going to put "When" and "the" on the same line. That means ungrouping "the" from "Sun Sets" and regrouping it with "When" which I'm also going to put in lower case to further de-emphasize it.

I'm going to center them, too. When I do that, I can see a green line through them like so:

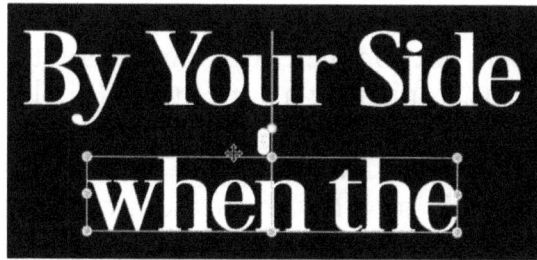

You can also see on that screenshot the distance between the two layers.

After some playing around with font sizes and alternates for the capital letters, here's my new layout.

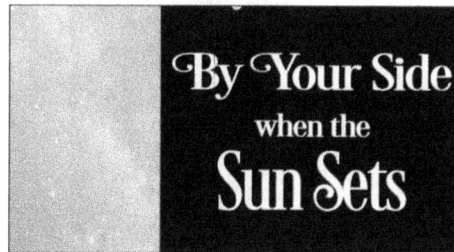

But I'm still not sold on it. You can see I used special versions for the "B", the "Y" and the "S" in sets. I tried to go with less ornate ones because this isn't that type of story.

But I think the last line is still dominating the space too much.

Here's another option to change the focus some:

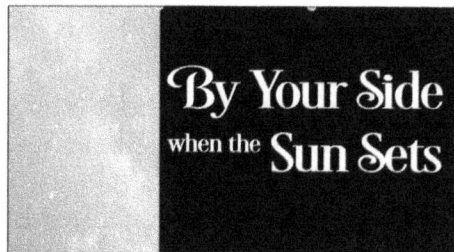

I like that better. But that many words on just two lines isn't going to work with our overall design. There's going to be way too much empty space when I zoom out and look at the entire cover. So even though this would work for a more normal cover where the text stretches across the entire width of the cover, it won't work here.

(Also, I noticed when I was working on this example that somehow the "By Your Side" and "Sun Sets portion were looking different even at the same font size, so I deleted Sun Sets, copied By Your Side and replaced the text with Sun Sets so they'd match up. I assume that was from resizing the font by clicking and dragging from the corner. Something to always be on the watch for.)

I'm not done yet, but right now I want to add my author name at the bottom of the cover so I can better see the whole layout.

I can't make it too large because it would pull the eye away from the title, so I think I should center it instead of left-align it.

See how there's just a lot of black space there between the title and the author name? I think it's too much.

And, honestly, coming back to this two weeks later after having to evacuate for a large wildfire, it's just kind of boring, isn't it? Like, eh, why would I download this?

(This is why it's always good to let things sit for a bit if you can before you publish them. I am definitely guilty of not doing that most times. I just get a wild hair to change a cover and put something together in a day and throw it up there. But if you can let things sit, you should. And if you can't, you should try to revisit them a month or so later.)

If that doesn't work, what other approach could we take to this?

This is what I originally came up with for this short story:

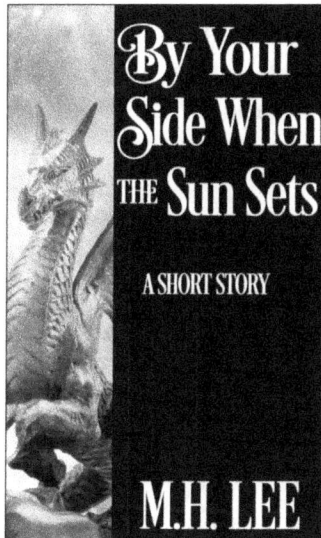

It certainly fills the space better, but that B is a bit too much and I really don't think the "the" needs to be so ornate and I'm kind of hating the alignment of the different text elements on the cover. I think I tried to left-align things and it just didn't work. And what is going on there with Short Story?

(I tell you, I fail in public more times than I can count…)

Here's another attempt:

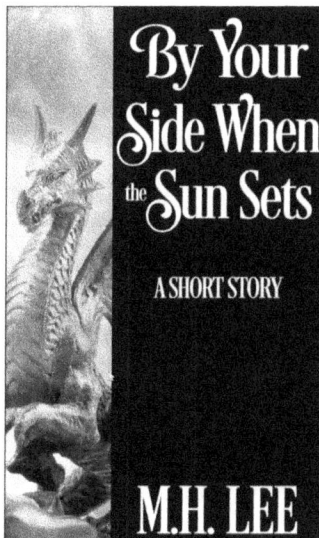

Better. I basically swapped out some of the first letters for different versions in Desire, centered the three lines of text instead of aligning them to the left, and made sure the vertical spacing between each section was the same. I also changed the "the" to a lower case, non-fancy version, and fixed whatever was going on with the short story line.

But I still don't like it.

Honestly, that title is shit. Don't do that to your cover designer. The more you can avoid little filler words like "by", "the", "of", etc. the better in my opinion. Unless it's a literary title.

So I'm going to poke at this a bit more. Maybe see if I can minimize that "by".

When I'm doing something like this, I drop each version I create into a folder and keep going. I will do this with different arrangements of the text, different fonts, different images, etc. and then at the end go look at all of the ideas I came up with side-by-side and pick the winners.

A trained designer would probably be able to do this instinctively without having to go through all the options, but for me it really helps to just try a lot of different approaches and then come back to them when I'm done. Usually what happens is that I end up with the third to last design or so out of twenty or thirty. The first few are crap, I start to narrow in on something that will work, but then I take it a little too far and have to backtrack.

Because the Affinity file thumbnails usually have a preview of the image on them, I always move the .jpg versions into their own folder called something like "images". Then as I compare them I rename them with a 1, 2, 3 etc. in front of the name to shuffle the images around and get them next to each other.

Like this:

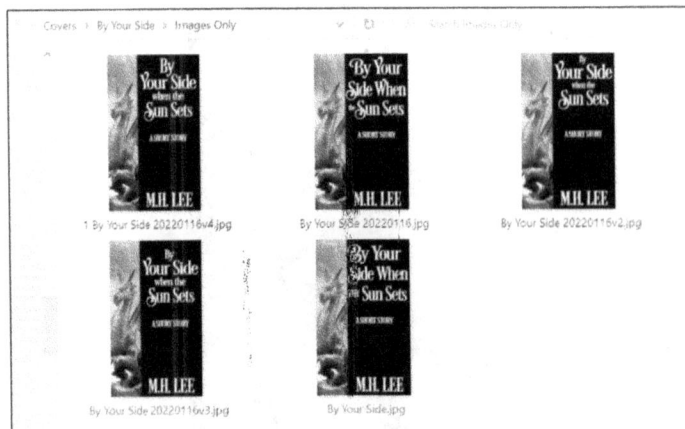

I think that first one there is a winner.

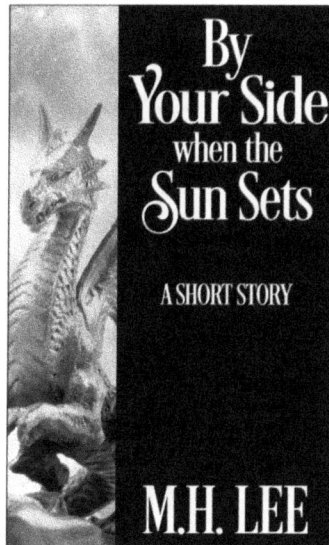

Or good enough for my purposes at least. And good enough for me to go swap that out for the existing one that's up there now.

That's the beauty of self-publishing, it's never too late to try something new and change things up.

(And because I use Vellum to do my own ebook interiors and this title is only out in ebook it takes maybe five minutes to update the ebook file and then the fifteen minutes or so to reload the new file on all the platforms.)

Okay, so we're done with that one for now. Next let's try a cover that uses a single image for the entire cover.

EBOOK COVER WITH A SINGLE IMAGE FOR THE ENTIRE COVER

Alright. Now it's time to create a cover where the entire cover is an image with text overlaid. Because this is basic cover design using Affinity Publisher there are certain tricks that I can't show you.

For example, you can use layer masks in Affinity Photo to blur out the background behind your text and make it more legible when you have a busy background. But that's in Photo not Publisher, so we can't do that.

Which means we have to be very smart about the image we choose for our cover or we need to use cheats like a band across a section of the cover.

First step is to find a good cover image. Many of the images on stock photo sites are good images when they're just sitting there on the screen, but they don't make for good cover images.

Remember when choosing an image that will fill the entire cover that you are working with a rectangular space, so one that's a portrait orientation is going to be better than one that's a landscape orientation. Also, if the entire image is busy, that's going to distract from your text.

Okay.

Let's go look at some examples. We're going to re-do that puppy cover from above, but with a full-cover image.

I'm going to use my Shutterstock images folder for this because the license on those images is one that lets me use them whenever whereas for Depositphotos I try to download images only as I use them due to the wording of their license terms.

This is what we have to choose from:

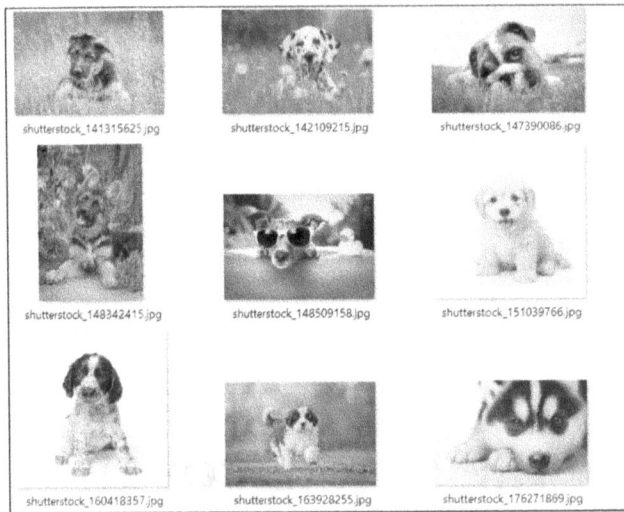

We have nine stock images here of puppies. The three in the top row as well as the one in the middle would be great choices for the design we used before. They all have bright colors and are landscape orientation so if we pop them into that design they're going to fit well and have an emphasis on the cute puppy.

But they're not ideal as-is for the type of cover we're going to do here because they don't have a lot of space above and below the puppy to place text. Also, especially with the images with grass in the background it's not easy to add on in a way that matches up with the details around the puppies.

The center one we could maybe pull off (and actually will later) because of the blue below, but it's still going to be tricky because it's not a solid blue.

The puppy in the second row on the left has the image orientation that will work and we can possibly fit some text in there at the bottom, but it would probably work better with more advanced design skills. In a situation like this I'd probably tend more towards one of the images with a white background even though that may have less "sophistication" to it.

If I'm not sure what will work, what I like to do is on the stock photo website right-click and save a copy of the images I'm considering to my desktop. I can then put them into my design and see which ones will actually fit the design before I go ahead and purchase the image I want. Yes, the image will be blurry because it's a thumbnail and there will likely be a watermark across it, but it at least lets me get a feel for whether that image has any chance of working.

Right now, though, I'm going to actually use one you don't see here which has two cute puppies in a flower pot and lots of nice white space above. It also uses a bright pink color, so less work for me. (You'll see it in just a minute, don't worry.)

Now that we have an image to work with, let's open Affinity Publisher and start a new book cover. I'm going to start from scratch with this one, no existing guide lines.

My next step is to place the image. I want this in a picture frame so that I can see the boundaries of what will show on my cover. So I start with the Picture Frame Rectangle Tool and use it to draw a rectangle that fits the entire dimensions of my cover.

After that I can go to the Place Image Tool on the left-hand side, navigate to the image I want to use, and select it. Since I'm using a picture frame it will try to fill that space as best as possible. Like this:

That's fine. But I think I actually want that image to be a little larger and repositioned some.

To do that, I can either expand the picture frame layer in the Layers studio to get to the underlying image, click on that image layer, and then go back to my workspace and make my adjustments.

Or I can use the slider below the picture frame to change the image size and click in the center of the four arrows in the center of the image to move it around that way. (Just be careful not to move the picture frame if you use that option. Ctrl + Z is your friend if you do.)

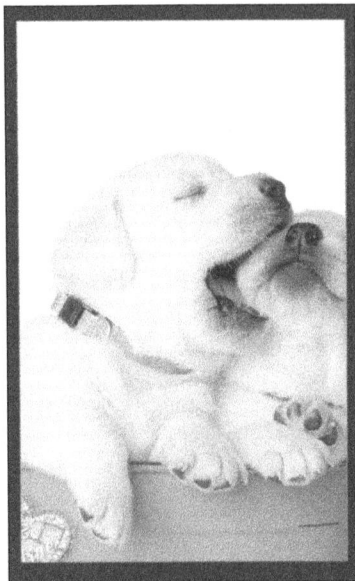

Better. But we have an issue, which is that we're working with an image that has a white background. It looks fine now, but it is going to be a problem when the image is displayed on Amazon and other ebook websites. The cover image will blend into the background so that it's not a distinct thumbnail. (Kind of like what happened with the cover thumbnail we used for the A+ content in the ad creative book where that fact was to our advantage.)

The solution to this is to place a very small light gray border around the cover. And good news. Because we used a picture frame, this should be relatively easy to do. If you don't use a picture frame then you basically need to make your image go not quite to the edge of the document and then you need to put a light gray rectangle layer behind it.

We have a picture frame, though, so let's go ahead and add our border real quick.

Click on the picture frame layer and then go to the dynamic menu up top where it shows Stroke and a line with a red slash next to it that says None.

Click on that line to bring up a border dropdown menu. Change the Width setting to something like .5. It doesn't have to be obvious, it just has to be enough to distinguish your cover from a white background.

The default right now is that the line will be black, but you can also click on that black color box next to Stroke in the dynamic menu and change it using the Swatches tab to a medium gray or even a light gray. Just something that isn't white.

Okay. So now we have an image with a border. Next we need text.

This is when you need to decide if this is a cover for a title that's part of a series or if it's a standalone. Because if it's standalone you can do whatever you want. Obviously, if you have an author brand you'll want to use some of that branding to keep consistency across your titles, even standalones, but you don't have to worry about placing the title and the author name in the same place each and every time.

For a series it really is a good idea to keep that consistent.

Go look at a bunch of authors on Amazon if you don't believe me. See which ones look the best to you in the series thumbnail listings they provide. I would bet you that consistent placement of author name and title really helps keep things looking like they belong together.

And I will tell you it's harder to get that consistency with stock images and using a full-cover image. The reason this series has the covers it does and not covers like the one we're about to create is because it was too hard to get good puppy images that would work well across thirteen covers and let me place my title and author name in the same place each time.

I actually started out with covers like this one and rebranded.

But let's pretend I have a bunch of images that will work. Or that I'm going to be able to pull off one of the other tricks people sometimes can do for a long series, which is that I'm going to stick with this exact image but will change out the pink color for other colors as I go forward. So the next one might be bright blue. The one after that a green. Then orange, etc.

This is a no-name author that readers will not recognize, so let's put the author name in the bottom right corner in a small font size.

I'm going to place this text directly on the workspace, so I use the Artistic Text Tool, click and drag an A in the bottom right corner and then type in the author name, "C. Coal".

It comes out as black, Arial, 25 pt. I want to change that to white and I'm going to use Fontin SmallCaps for my font. So, Ctrl + A to select all and then I can make my changes up top.

Once I do that I adjust the font size and move the text around until I'm happy with it.

Ideally I'd probably want my text a little larger than it is, but I'm dealing with a black line on the image that I don't want to overlap. And since this is Publisher not Photo I don't have good tools for erasing that black line.

I'm going to try a simple layout with Puppy Love in Fontin SmallCaps and then Spring Fling in some sort of scrawled cursive. So I add Puppy Love as one layer and Spring and Fling as their own layers.

I then want Spring and Fling to be in a pink that matches the container the dogs are in, so I use the eyedropper option to grab that color.

At this point I'll go through all of my fonts looking for something that works for that cursive, hate every single one I have for being too lightweight or having a weird p I can't stand, or just otherwise not working, despair that I should've handed this over to a professional but know that would've cost more than the short story will ever make, and then finally settle on something that's okay.

Depending on the day and my mood I may save down about a dozen versions of the cover to compare them side-by-side.

In this case I ended up going with a font called Black Pillow that I didn't find too obnoxious and that at least gives that playful flair to the cover that matches the stories.

I used the rotate option to angle the word "Spring" and then changed the R value in the Transform studio for "Fling" to the same value to make sure that both layers were rotated at the same angle.

And here we go:

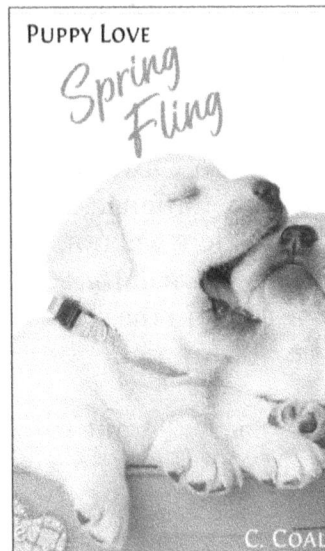

I had to move the image around a bit and it now bumps up against my author name in the bottom corner more than I'd like, but I put my guide lines on there to check and I like where they fall for the puppies, so it is what it is.

I think if I had to use this for a series I could do so without a lot of issues. It would probably work best if I kept the same image and swapped out the colors, although doing that successfully would be more of an intermediate-level design skill.

But let's see if I can just swap out the image here using the Document->Resource Manager option.

Let me go bring in another puppy image that has a white background, change the color for the author name text in the bottom, and done:

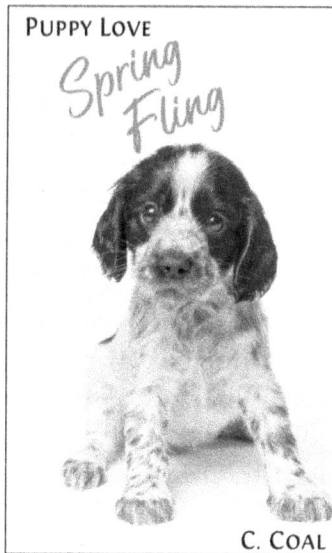

It works.

If I were designing this series of covers this way from scratch I'd probably drop the puppies in the flower pot and go more with images like this simply because it would give me better consistency across the entire series. I like the puppies in the flower pot more, but there just aren't enough images like them that I could successfully use.

So cover design is kind of like playing pool or chess, you need to be thinking a few moves ahead if you don't want to end up rebranding your covers later.

Alright. So that worked, but let's go back and do a different option.

We're going to choose an image that has no white space in it. But that means image choice becomes even more important.

Here I've brought in that cute chaos puppy with all the background detail.

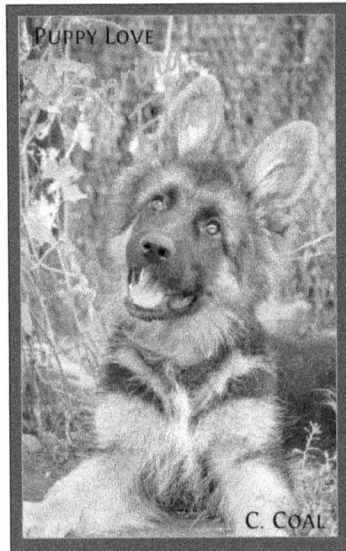

PUPPY LOVE

C. COAL

See how our text has disappeared into the detail? Sometimes if the detail isn't too extreme you can fix this with a contrasting color. But here I don't think that will work, so we'd need color blocks to place our text on.

A lot of times I'll just do a solid line across the bottom or the middle for this. Because, again, we're talking about basic covers here.

But I want to try something different on this one. I want to try to create angled shapes below the pup's face that I can then place my text on.

First things first, insert a small rectangle using the Rectangle Tool.

Theoretically you can then shear the rectangle by clicking near the sides and dragging, but I wasn't able to get that to work. So I went for alternative two, which is to use the Transform studio and change the S value.

Here is a rectangle with an S value of -40 degrees:

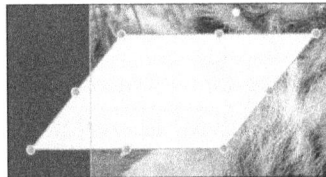

That turns out to be too much to go with the text we want to use, so I ended up dialing it back to -25 degrees when I saw the text on it. Which conveniently matches the angle I already had for the text.

It took me some experimenting back and forth to get the rectangle the right size because the "g" in each word takes up a lot of height.

Also, this seems to work best when each word is on its own rectangle and each one has a different background color. Remember, the background color of a rectangle can be changed using the Fill section in the dynamic menu at the top.

When I changed the rectangle color I also had to change the text color for one of my words to white.

And I decided I liked the shapes better when they overlap instead of being separate.

As a final step, I dragged the text layers onto the rectangle layers in the Layers studio so that they were sub-layers of each rectangle.

I then grouped the two rectangles together and used the Align Center option to center the group.

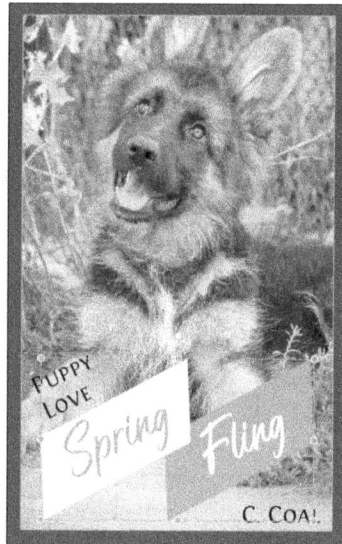

We're just looking at the Spring Fling portion here. I like how the sheared rectangles turned out with the text. I'm not sure I like the image I used because it doesn't go with the colors we've been using for this "brand".

If this was a standalone cover, I might just change the colors. If this was a series, I'd probably choose another image.

So let's do that now. Let's swap out our image for something brighter and cleaner:

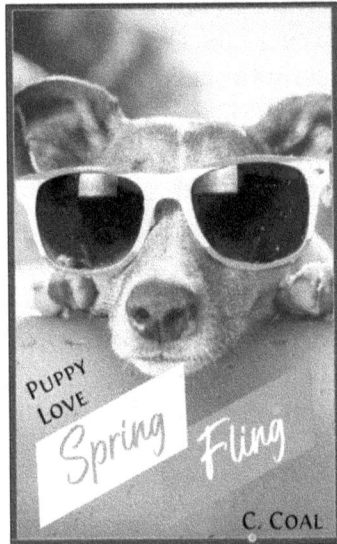

Much better.

I still need to fix the author name and series name, though.

Author name I can just make white. Series name I'm going to change to Black Pillow to match the title text and then put on one line and make white.

But that still leaves me the issue of the image. At the size I want it, the image doesn't go to the bottom of the page. See the white space down there?

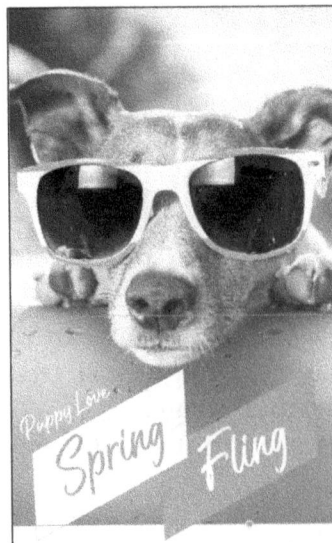

One possible trick for fixing this is to duplicate that image layer, so right-click in the Layers studio and choose Duplicate, and then flip it and line it up with the original.

To flip an image, go to Layer->Transform->Flip Vertical. Once you do that you can click and drag the image down until the two edges line up.

I also want to Align Horizontally using the options up top and then Group the two and reposition my dog in the center of the cover once more.

When I grouped the two images the X from the picture frame reappeared on top of them. To get rid of it—because it would have been visible in the final product—I had to ungroup them after I'd moved them to their final location.

And here's the final:

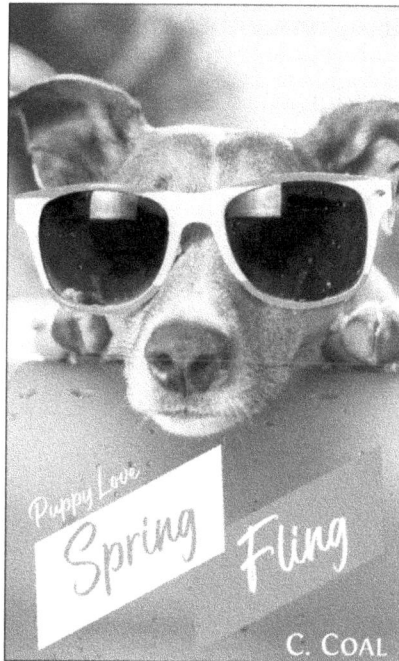

If we had put the title text straight on the image it would've probably been a little lost, but by putting those sheared rectangles behind the text we were able to make the text stand out.

Also, it's not ideal to have to duplicate and flip an image layer like we did here. Someone looking really close would probably be able to see the line where that happened, but for an ebook thumbnail cover it should be just fine.

And sometimes, depending on what's at the edge of an image, that won't work. But often with an image where things are subtly changing from light to dark like we have here that's a quick and dirty way to line things up so that the transition is more subtle than trying to use a solid color or trying to copy and cut a section and paste it onto the bottom.

I just want to emphasize one last time that the key with using a full image is making sure that the image you choose works well for a book cover. And if it's for a series you have to remember that it gets much trickier to use full images because every image you choose has to work with all of the series design elements, including placement and colors if you go that direction.

But the nice thing about using a full image like this is it can give depth to your cover that you won't have otherwise. Here we have water drops on a blue surface and the hint of a background behind the dog whereas the cover we did earlier that had white space to work with really didn't have that depth.

As with all covers, though, remember that you're ultimately trying to sell a product. So at the end of the day the question is, does this work for selling this book to the right kind of reader? If the answer is no, then it's the wrong cover no matter how beautiful it is.

Okay. On to print covers.

KDP PAPERBACK COVER

Now let's walk through how to take an existing ebook cover and turn it into a paperback cover using a solid background.

So, again, this is not the fancy, high-end "wow" sort of print cover where the image wraps around the entire cover, but more the basic, functional, gets the job done type.

One of the mistakes I made early on with print covers and still do to some extent, is that I failed to appreciate the variance in the print-on-demand process.

What do I mean by this? I mean that I would put a border around a cover, like this:

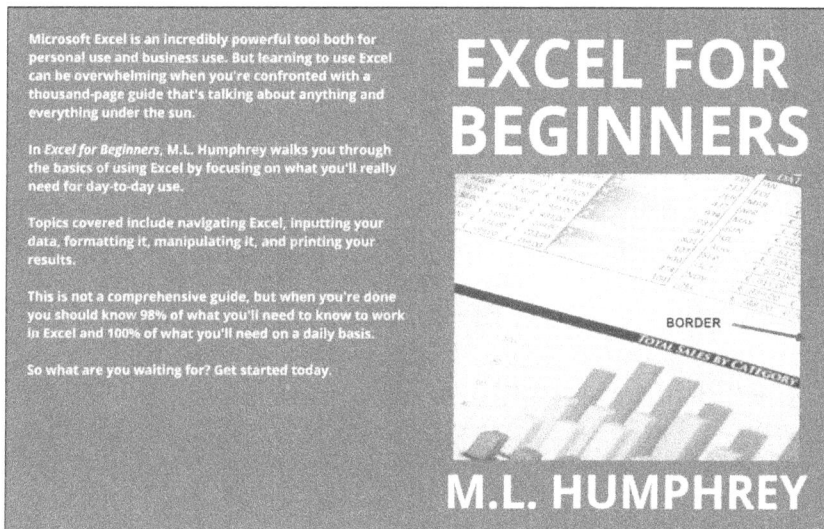

And I would fail to realize that sometimes that blue border on the right-hand side was going to be only an eighth of an inch and sometimes it was going to be a quarter of an inch and it could fall anywhere in between. Which meant that sometimes that cover looks lopsided when it prints.

Now, this book has sold a lot of copies with that cover and has decent reviews, so most readers don't seem too freaked out about it, but it annoys me.

Which is why you'll notice that the ebook covers I showed you in this book don't follow that layout. The images we used either cover the entire space, the left-hand side of the space, or the entire cover from left-to-right. That's how I now get around this issue.

My cozy covers still have a central image in them, but if you look back at the one I showed you in the beginning it's a central image that's so confined to the center of the cover that this edge issue doesn't come into play because most of the cover is a solid color.

I mention this because I want you to be aware of this issue when you do your own cover designs. Hopefully I can help you avoid at least one of the mistakes I have made. (And hopefully more than one by the time we're done here.)

Okay. So let's take that fantasy short story cover we put together earlier and use it to create a print cover.

We're going to do this for KDP paperback, IngramSpark paperback, and IngramSpark hard cover. I always start with the KDP paperback cover, so that's what we'll do here as well.

I am also, so that we have enough spine to work with, going to pretend that this is a full novel we're doing this for.

(If a book is too short there is no spine text allowed as you can actually see on the image above for *Excel for Beginners*. That one, quirkily enough, is at a length that it does have spine text on the IngramSpark version but not on the KDP version.)

First step, we need a template. There is no reason ever for you to create a print cover from absolute scratch. (And also no reason to ever pay for a bar code.)

To get the KDP template, go to the KDP website (https://kdp.amazon.com/ en_US/), and click on Help at the top of the screen. In the search bar type, "Create a Paperback Cover" and then click on that help topic. Scroll down on that page that comes up to where there is some blue text that says "cover calculator and template generator," and click on it.

As of right now, that brings up something that looks like this:

Print Cover Calculator and Templates

To find out the exact dimensions of your cover, use the calculator. You can also download a template (PDF and PNG) to be used as a guide layer in your image editing software. Learn more about Hardcover and Paperback cover requirements.

Enter Your Book Information

Binding type
Select one

Interior type
Select one

Paper type
Select one

Page-turn direction
Select one

Measurement units
Select one

Interior trim size
Select one

Page count
Number of pages at your formatted trim size.
Learn more about trim size and page count

Calculate dimensions

Download Template

Reset book information

I say "as of right now" because this is not what it looked like a year ago and, knowing Amazon, it may not look this way a year from now. They changed all of this when they added hard covers as a print option. Plus, sometimes they just like to change things up so that every guide about how to work with them becomes hopelessly outdated. (Ask me how I know…)

But as long as you know that there are print templates available through their help option you should be able to find and download them. That at least has remained consistent for the last eight or so years.

Anyway. Get to this screen or find the template generator somehow and then tell Amazon what kind of print book you want to create.

You will need to know a few things about your book before you can do this.

First, you need to know how many pages the interior file is going to be. (This means formatted, not just what Word says when you're done. And it includes all front and back matter. So you need the interior done before you can finalize your cover.)

You also need to know what size you want the book to be.

A personal pet peeve of mine is people who use 6 x 9 for paperbacks. I have many, many, many trade published books on my shelves and they are generally not that size in paperback.

In general, for fiction, 6 x 9 is for hard covers. I do have some 6 x 9 fiction paperbacks, but they tend to be either omnibuses—so multiple books in one print edition—or something like a "best of" collection. They are generally not individual titles. The only time I personally use 6 x 9 is for my large print titles.

Also, if you're self-publishing you're probably not creating a mass market title either, which is the smaller print size you can find in bookstores.

What you are likely going to be creating is a trade paperback, which is the larger paperback size that so many books come in these days. So you're looking in the five-inch range not the four- or six- inch range.

If you want to fit in on the shelves with other print books in your genre then go to the library or go to the bookstore and measure some books. (Or bring a bunch of books up on Amazon and look for their print measurements there.)

I personally use 5.25 x 8 for regular print titles. I know others who use 5.5 x 8.5. This is in inches. KDP does give a millimeters option if you want to go that route and are more used to those measurements because you're not in the U.S. so where you are they use slightly different sizes. (Although I'd keep in mind there where you think you'll sell most of your copies and try to choose a size that works for your target market.)

Also, you need to know what kind of paper you want to use because that will impact how wide the spine of your book is. This can also impact the choices you have for trim size.

On KDP you can choose white or cream paper. IngramSpark also offers a groundwood paper option now.

Unless you're doing some sort of fancy, high-priced edition, you're not going to do color. For POD it just costs too much to be feasible and they don't care if it's just one colored page in your book. Any color other than black and white costs lots to print on demand.

The spine width of the KDP template will change with each increment of ten pages. On IngramSpark they're more exact about it and they go down to the exact page count.

Once you know all of that, enter your information, like so:

Next, click on Calculate Dimensions followed by Download Template. This will download a zip file to your computer that contains a PNG file as well as a PDF. I've always worked with the PDF version.

To be able to open the PDF with Affinity, open the zip file, copy the PDF, and paste it outside of the zip file.

Now you're ready to actually work on your cover in Affinity Publisher.

Open Affinity, close out any pop-ups or welcome screens, and then go to File -> Open and navigate to where you placed the PDF cover template.

Click on the file and then click Open. This will bring up the PDF Options dialogue box:

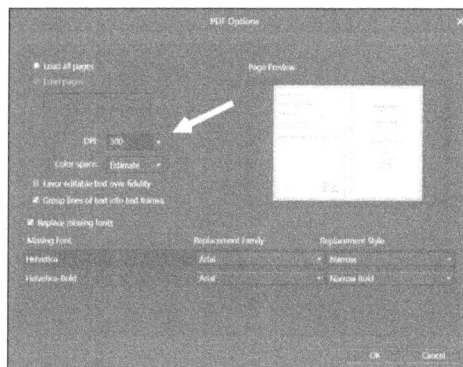

Now. This is key. And it's a mistake I made in GIMP, which is the program I used before this, which screwed up my covers.

You *must* import the PDF file at 300 DPI or more. If you do not do so and you later try to export at 300 DPI, it won't work. You can't fix this after the fact. Garbage in, garbage out.

Also, it won't matter that you added text while you were in the program or that you used a high resolution image, because whatever you import this template at is what will govern all of the elements you put on that cover.

So if you import at 100 DPI, which I think was GIMP's default, that's what all of the elements will be set to. Which will make your spine text blurry at small sizes and your images more muddied.

(Ask me how I know.)

So make sure your DPI value is 300 before you click OK.

Now. The way that Affinity Publisher imports a PDF is it breaks all of the components of the PDF into separate layers. (As opposed to GIMP which imports it as one layer.)

Which means the first thing I do when that file imports is I go to the Layers studio, click on a layer, use Ctrl + A to select all of the layers, and then use Ctrl + G to group them. That reduces all of that noise down to one layer group.

At this point, you should have something that looks like this:

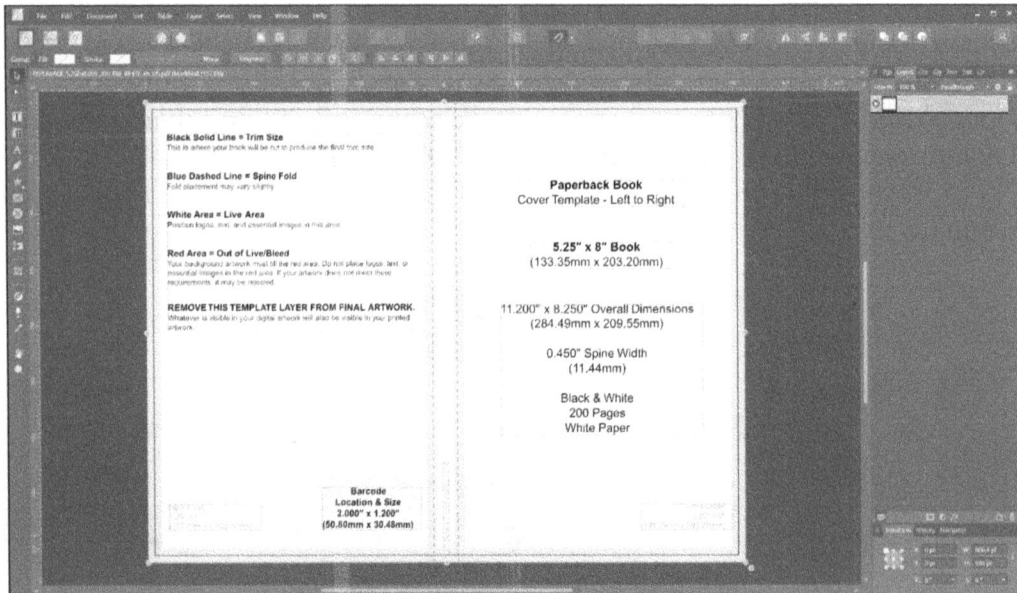

If you want to, you can delete the descriptive text layers from the template. Sometimes I can ignore them, sometimes they annoy me. This time around I'm going to delete them.

To do so, I expand the group I created from the PDF layers, click on the first layer that has a text description (Spine Width…), hold down the shift key and click on the last layer that has a text description (Paperback Book Cover…).

I then use the Delete key which leaves me with just the rectangles that delineate each space. Like so:

Much easier to work with.

My next step is to add the solid-colored background. I'm going to use the fantasy cover we did earlier so I'm going to add a black background.

To do that, I go to the Rectangle Tool on the left-hand side, click and drag to cover the template, and then change the cover to black using the Swatches tab after clicking on the Fill box in the dynamic menu up top.

Remember that it's sometimes easier to add a rectangle by clicking and drawing it within the space first and then dragging each edge to the perimeter of the space. If you have snapping enabled you'll see green or red lines as you do that.

Because I need to see the template for the other layers, I immediately uncheck the box for the rectangle I just added in the Layers studio to hide it for the time being.

Now I can bring in the ebook cover.

The simplest way to do so is to click on the Place Image Tool, navigate to where the cover JPG I created is stored, and then click and drag on the white space on the right-hand side to place the cover.

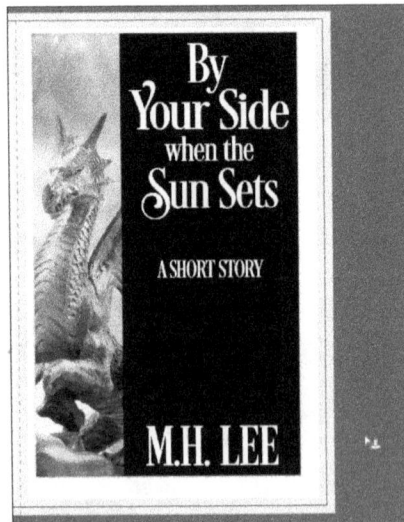

It is not going to fit perfectly.

Place it in as much of the white space as you can manage. Given the cover dimensions I used and the print size I chose, I can fit my cover in the white space with just a little bit of white showing on the left- and right-hand sides.

Keep the cover within the white space because this is the space that is guaranteed to print. The pink space on the right edge and top and bottom is what may or may not print. The pink space on the left edge may end up on the spine.

That's the quick and dirty way to do this. The advantage is that you don't have to mess with each individual item that was on the ebook cover. They're all set where they need to be compared to one another.

But the disadvantage is that I'm going to have a black border on the left of the dragon image and at the top and bottom.

It'll look something like this:

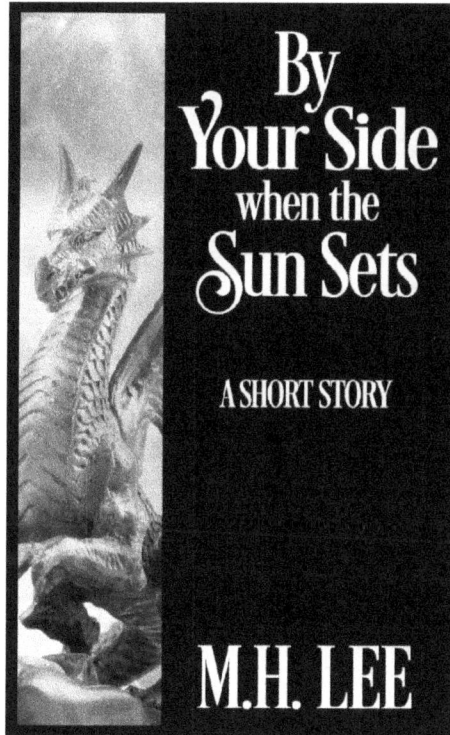

Which is fine. I'm generally okay with that and would probably do this cover that way.

But you may not be.

If you aren't, then what you need to do is bring in the cover elements separately. So delete the layer with the ebook cover that we just created here for our print file, and then go and open the Affinity Publisher file for the ebook cover.

Note, this is the Affinity Publisher file not the JPG file.

In that file, select all of the layers except for Master A and your background. Copy them using Ctrl + C. Click over to your print template and paste them using Ctrl + V. It'll look something like this:

(If you don't like that you can also copy in the background so all of the elements are more visible when you paste them in. It can just cause issues later if you ever change the background for the print book because you'll also have this background layer for the front cover section that's separate and will also need to be changed.)

When you pasted in the layers from the ebook cover, they will still be grouped together. And will also generally paste onto the left-hand side of the template.

Left-click and drag to move the entire group to the right-hand white space for the front cover. You may also need to resize the grouped layers from the corner to fit them into the space.

Also, make sure the layers pasted in above your background layer. If not, go to the Layers studio and move the group or the background layer so that the background layers is lower.

You can always turn on the rectangle layer to see how white text that's not currently showing well will look:

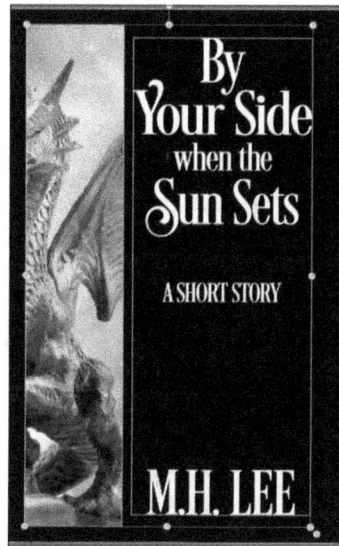

The problem now is the need to work with white text on a white background while making sure that the individual elements stay in good alignment with one another and the template.

I want to see the elements in the template that are behind my black background, but I also want to see the text I'm working with.

What I can do is click on the black rectangle layer in the Layers studio, make sure it's checked so it's visible, but change its opacity to about 70%. I've done that here:

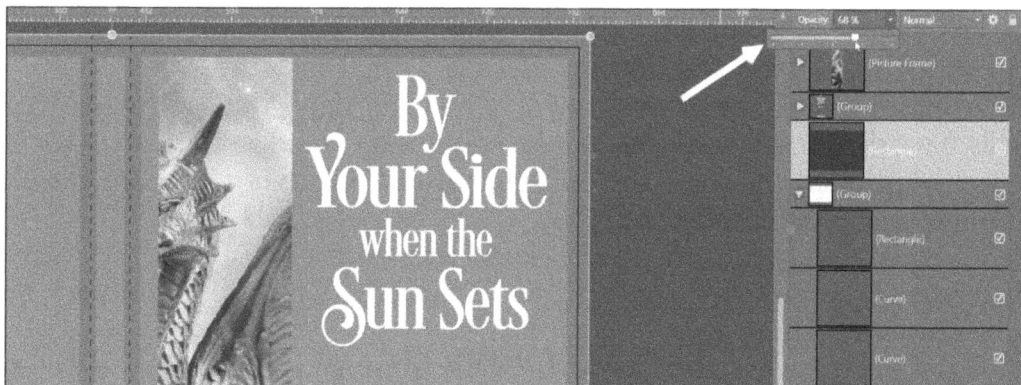

Note how I can now see the white text and also see the template parameters?

I'll need to change this opacity setting back at the end, but this lets me work with my white text and the template at the same time.

The reason we did all of this was to extend the picture frame for the image on the front cover. So let's click on that picture frame in the Layers studio and then go to the canvas and extend the frame all the way to the top and bottom edge of the template. Let's also extend it to the dotted line along the spine.

After I do that I also need to reposition my image in the frame.

That gives me a cover that will look something like this:

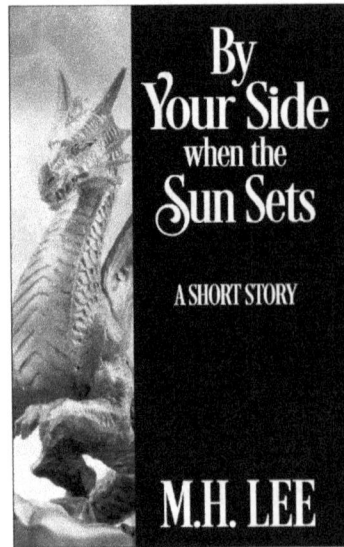

This is print on demand, so it's not guaranteed that I won't have a little bit of black creeping around the edge of the spine there, but at least I won't have to worry about uneven top and bottom edges if I do it this way.

We're not going to do it here, but if I had the right kind of image I could actually have that image wrap around the spine and extend all the way to the back edge of the print cover. That's the only guaranteed way to not have any problems with the image and the spine.

Problem is, though, I'd then have spine text on the image and I'd probably need to use some more advanced tricks to make my spine text and back cover copy visible over that image.

And no matter what you do with POD printing you'll always have some variance somewhere.

So we're just going with black spine and black back cover and doing the best we can.

Which means the next step we have is to add our back cover copy. Click on the Frame Text Tool and then click and drag on the white space for the back cover to create a box where you can place your back cover copy.

I don't take the text frame to the edges of the space, which means I try to place my text frame so that it's centered in the white space on the back cover and has an equal amount of white on the left and right sides.

Again, this is POD so there's going to be some variance each time the cover prints so even if you get it perfectly centered there is no guarantee it will print that way every time.

Once the text frame is in position, click on the Artistic Text Tool and then into the frame and add your back cover copy. I copied mine from a Word document so it pasted in black and in Arial 11.2 pt. Which meant the next step was to select all (Ctrl + A) and change the font, font color, and font size.

I also decided to center my text because there wasn't a lot of it. I would've liked to bold and italicize the top line, but because I was using the Desire font I didn't have those weight options to work with.

But here it is:

What do you do when your best friend is three stories tall, breathes fire, and may be forgetting that you're his friend?

Find out in this short story about an aging dragonrider and his dragon.

You can obviously get more fancy with your back cover. You can put in an author photo and bio, for example. Or a review blurb or two. Whatever you want to put there. For text, I recommend using the text frames. For photos I'd use the Picture Frame Rectangle Tool.

On the KDP template you do not need to include a bar code, they put it in there for you. That yellow rectangle on the template marks where it will go. Don't put anything important in that space. It's fine if your background image goes across that space, but they'll reject the cover if your author bio or something like that encroaches on that space.

Next up and the final element is the spine text.

This one I do not use a text frame for, although you could.

I just click on the Artistic Text Tool and then click on or about the spine and type in the title.

(You may need to click and drag to create an A before you can start typing. That just happened to me, but it doesn't always so it could've been down to whatever tool I had selected just beforehand.)

I try to keep my spine text in all caps because it makes positioning the text in the center of the spine easier.

My text was in Arial and in black so I needed to select all and change that as well.

Next, I need to rotate the text so it fits on the spine.

To do so, go to Layer->Transform->Rotate Right. That should rotate your text to vertical with the tops of the letters on the right. (If you were doing a book in Spanish or other languages where spine text faces the other way, you'd want to go the other direction.)

Click and drag the text layer back to the spine.

It needs to fit within the white space on the spine. In my case the text was too big, so I had to select all of the text and change the font size.

It's a good idea to leave a little bit of white space on both sides of your text, because, again, POD variation is going to potentially shift things about a little bit and if you're right up against the margins that may cause your spine text to look really awkward. (I don't think it would actually wrap around to the front or back cover, but it would probably go right up to the edge.)

When you upload the template you'll also see that Amazon's review page has very bright red lines showing where you cannot have spine text.

Okay.

Once the text is the right size, you can move that layer to the position along the spine that you want.

I tend to put my title towards the top and my author name towards the bottom. If you have a series, try to position your text starting at the same spot on each cover so that they line up nicely on the shelf.

(Another one I have messed up in the past. But looking at my shelves, I'm not alone in that.)

Once you position the title, you can right-click on that layer in the Layers studio and Duplicate, then click into the canvas and drag it down to about where you want your author name.

Make sure the text tool is selected and then click onto the dragged-down layer and replace the text with the author name. Adjust your positioning as needed.

Since the KDP template has nothing added outside of the cover itself (unlike IngramSpark, which we'll see in a minute) you can have Affinity center your spine text for you. Just click on each layer and use the Align Center, Align Horizontally menu option at the very top.

At this point it's a good idea to check that you don't have a bottom-heavy font or a font that in some way doesn't easily center. To do that, zoom in on your spine text. (View->Zoom->400%)

This one looks pretty good to me. If it didn't, I'd either manually adjust or choose a different font.

Zoom the view back (View->Zoom->Zoom to Width or sometimes Zoom to Fit), change the rectangle layer to 100% opacity, and that should be it.

At this point you could delete the group that has the template layers in it, but since they're completely covered by the background layer we added, you don't have to.

I tend not to because if I want to make tweaks later I want those template layers there to guide me.

Next step is to export as a PDF. Go to File->Export and choose the PDF option.

For KDP you need to be able to export *with bleed* or you'll get an error message that the file isn't the right size.

The "PDF (press ready)" option lets you do this, so select it from the dropdown men. Also make sure that the DPI is set to a minimum of 300.

For a cover you want the whole document. And I usually check to preview when complete.

And here is our final cover PDF:

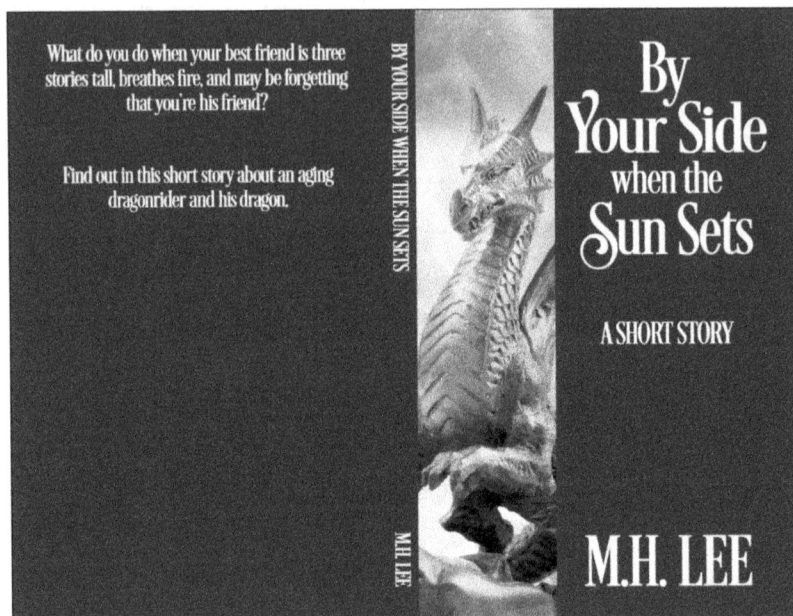

A basic print cover with the ebook cover image (adjusted in this case to remove a top or bottom black border possibility), spine text with the title and author name, and basic back cover copy.

Keep in mind that if this were a real short story cover the template wouldn't have shown a white space on the spine because for short books (under about 110 pages) Amazon doesn't allow spine text. The white space in each template is all that you have to work with for placing your key elements, so if there isn't white space you can't add text to the spine.

Okay. Now on to IngramSpark covers.

INGRAMSPARK PAPERBACK COVER

Next up is taking the print cover we just created and turning it into an IngramSpark (IS) paperback cover.

This needs to be a separate step because the template that IS uses is different from the KDP template. And there are slight differences in terms of spine width between the two platforms so the covers are not in fact interchangeable.

But it doesn't take too long.

First thing is to get your IS template. Go to the IngramSpark Cover Template Generator, currently found at https://myaccount.ingramspark.com/Portal/Tools/CoverTemplateGenerator and input your information.

If you have already set up your book on IS through to the upload step then most of this information will automatically populate for you when you input the ISBN.

But if you haven't yet, you'll have to manually enter it.

The file type I select is PDF.

I used to include price in the bar code because as a former bookstore employee I'm used to being able to quickly glance at the bar code on a book and see the price there. But since IS has become a lot more tight-fisted about update codes and has started raising their prices on a more regular basis in the last year, I think I'm probably going to stop doing that. Most of my sales are online anyway.

So fill the form out, hit submit, and you should receive an email with the PDF in it within a few minutes.

You do have to have a valid ISBN for them to generate the template. Above I tried to just make one up and it gave me an error message.

So for this next step I'm going to actually use a template I already have that was for a two-hundred-page book. The concept of what we're about to do won't change if I use an old file. It's just the ISBN on the template that's going to be different.

First step, as before, is to open the PDF file in Affinity, making sure that under PDF Options it's coming in as a 300 DPI image.

(I should note here that I always have it estimate the color space, but if you're doing something fancy with your covers then you should probably set that to CMYK.)

This is what a typical paperback template from IngramSpark looks like:

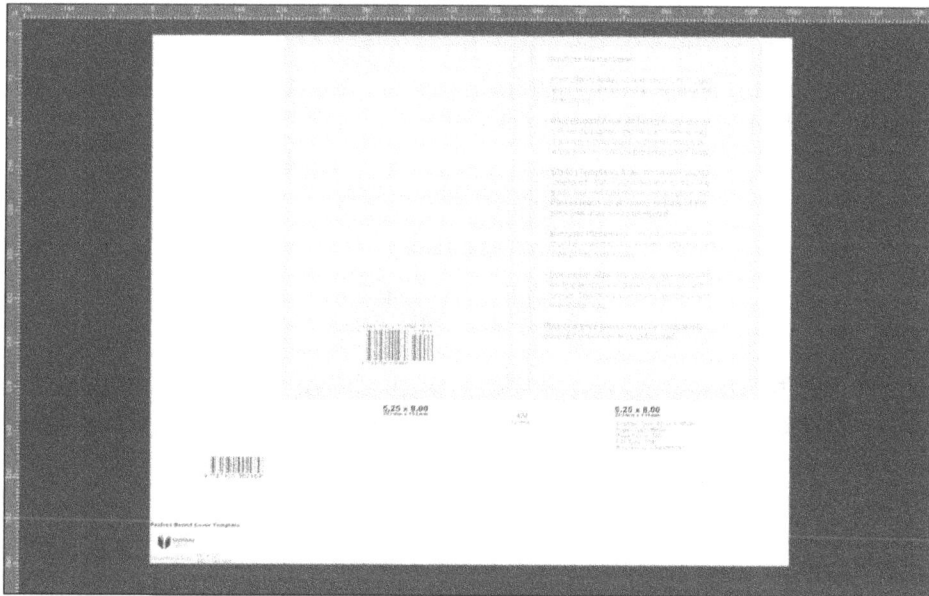

Note how the actual cover portion is just part of the template. And in this case, the areas where you can put key text and images is pink and the areas that may get cut off or caught on the edge of the spine are blue.

You can also see that the template comes with a bar code on the back cover. This is why you never need to pay for one, because you can always generate an IngramSpark template and use the bar code from there. The bar code is specific to the ISBN you provided.

Below the image it shows the trim size of the book, the details about the book formatting like page count, and the book ISBN. They will reject a cover file that has the wrong ISBN on it.

If you change any of the information you can see on this template, you need to generate a new template and create a new cover. And if you have already published the book and change the title, author, type of paper, or interior color that requires a new ISBN.

Okay. So getting back to the cover design.

The first thing I do when I import the IS template is I group all of the PDF layers. Just like we did with the KDP template. So Layers studio, click on a layer, Ctrl + A, Ctrl + G.

Next I turn the bar code layers into their own group.

The nice thing is that the bar code is the first three layers in the template. So expand that group you just created in the Layers studio, select the first three layers (using Shift or Ctrl to select multiple layers at once), and then use Ctrl + G to group those first three layers into their own subgroup.

Next, left-click and drag that bar code group you just created above the larger group that has all of the PDF layers. Like so:

You'll still need to drag the bar code group above the background layer in a minute for it to be visible, but this at least gets it into its own separate layer where you can be reminded to do that. (And if you forget, which I do on occasion, IngramSpark seems to add one for you. I know there are times I've forgotten but the proof showed a bar code.)

Now that we're done with getting the template sorted, we're ready to bring in all of the elements we used for the KDP cover.

Open the KDP cover Affinity file and select all of the layers except the Group layer you created of the KDP PDF template. Ctrl + C to copy, click back over to the IS template, and Ctrl + V to paste.

As it did with the ebook cover when we pasted that in, Affinity tends to paste things to the top left corner by default.

Everything will still be grouped at this point, so you can easily left-click and drag the group over to cover the section of the IS template that is meant for the cover.

I try to drag the cover into place so that the top and at least one side show my alignment lines as you can see here with this close-up of the top left corner where I have both a green and a red alignment line showing:

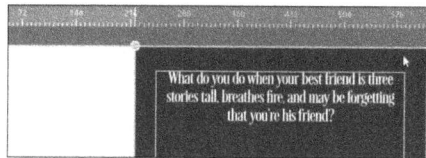

That may be hard to see in print. My apologies.

At this point I click onto the Rectangle layer in the Layers studio so that I'm only dealing with my background layer, and I click and drag from each side and from the top and bottom to make sure that my background is covering the area on the template devoted to the cover.

So I will either click and drag out and back in or in and back out until I see those red or green lines.

It's a bit redundant since I'd already lined up two sides. I could have just done the other two sides and been fine, but I do it that way anyway.

And, actually, the KDP and IS templates should be the same size top to bottom, it's the width that's slightly different. But still.

Okay. Next step is to hide that layer. So click on the box next to the Rectangle layer in the Layers studio. Your canvas should now look something like this:

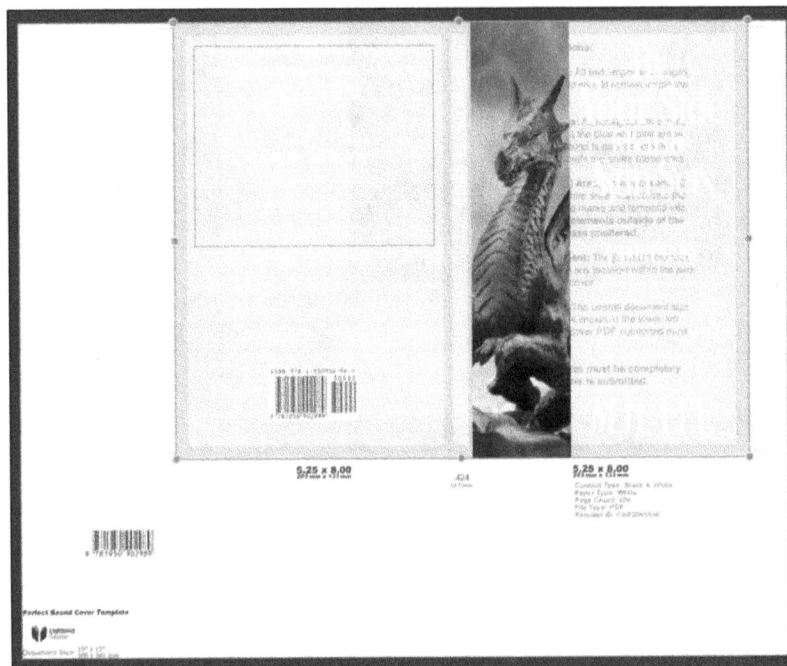

What you're looking for here is that the back cover copy is still centered, that the spine text is centered, and that the front cover elements still fall in the main cover space without issue or need for adjustment.

You will almost always need to adjust the spine text.

Often I have to adjust the back cover copy frame. This time it looks okay, though. Maybe it could go a smidge to the right.

If I want to be exact, there's a layers trick I can use with the IS template that doesn't work with the KDP template. And that's to pull up a specific layer from the PDF template elements to right below the layer I'm trying to place. This lets me see the distance for the layer I'm trying to place compared to that portion of the template.

(If you don't do this you'll notice that Affinity gives you a distance but it's not always to where you want. It might be to the edge of the template instead of the edge of the pink space on the back cover, for example.)

Let's do this for the spine text.

First step. Go to the group for the PDF template and expand it and then scroll down until you find the thin pink vertical layer that represents the spine text.

Click on that layer and then go to the gray and yellow square images in the topmost area of the workspace and find the one that says "Move to Front":

Click on that and it should move the spine layer up to the top of the group. You can then easily click and move it the rest of the way up to just below the spine text layer.

Here is the Layers studio with it moved up to just below the title and author name layers for the spine:

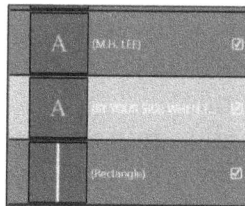

Next step is to Zoom in to 400% or so and then move around until you can see the title on the spine. Here we can clearly see that the title is no longer centered:

But Affinity can't center this for us against the overall template like it did for the KDP template, because the cover on the template is not centered. What we can do, though, is click on the title layer and use the left and right arrows to move the title until the values showing on the right and left-hand side of the title are the same.

Because we moved the pink spine area up right below our title and author layers, the distance that's being shown by Affinity is the distance to the edges of the pink spine area. If we hadn't move that up it would be using different reference points on the left and right sides that were not equidistant from the spine.

You can either do the same thing for the author name or you can use the Transform studio to give that layer the same X value as the title layer.

Zoom back out and move the pink spine layer back below the background layer. It doesn't have to return to where you found it, just move it so that it's no longer visible in your final document.

While you're in the Layers studio, drag the bar code group layer up above the background layer and then go to your workspace and position the bar code where you want it. I usually place it in the bottom right corner of the back cover, so I drag it over and down a bit.

Finally, click on the checkbox for the background layer in the Layers studio to turn it back on.

And that should be it. You should now have your IS paperback cover ready to go.

Export as PDF. This time as PDF/X-1a:2003, which seems to work with IS. You want the whole document but you do not need to include bleed this time around.

And this is what you upload to IngramSpark, extra white space, text, and all.

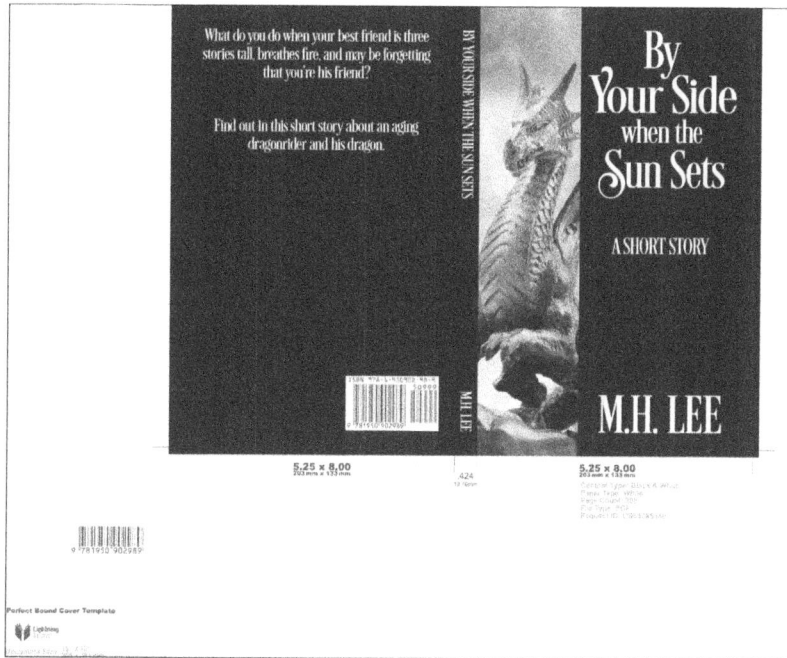

When you get back your print proof from IS, though, do be sure to zoom in on the PDF file to check your text on your spine.

You can see the dotted lines that extend down from the spine. You want to make sure that no text falls outside of those lines.

Also, be sure there's no blue from the template peeking through along the edges of your image. A pixel worth or so is probably going to be fine, but too much and you run the risk that print variance will sometimes put a white trim along the edge of your cover.

(Even when you get this right, that can still happen if it's a bad print run.)

Okay. One more cover to go, the IngramSpark case laminate hard cover version. It requires more work, but is much the same as what we just did for the paperback.

INGRAMSPARK CASE LAMINATE HARD COVER

The first step is to go back to the cover template generator on the IS website and generate your cover template.

The type of cover we're doing here is a case laminate cover, which means that there is no removable wraparound cover. It prints directly onto the binding just like a paperback cover does.

Unfortunately, perhaps, for hard cover you can't use the same size we just used, it's not available. So this time around we're going to work with a 6 x 9 cover.

So get your template and open it just like we've done before. And make sure it comes in at 300 DPI.

This is what it looks like:

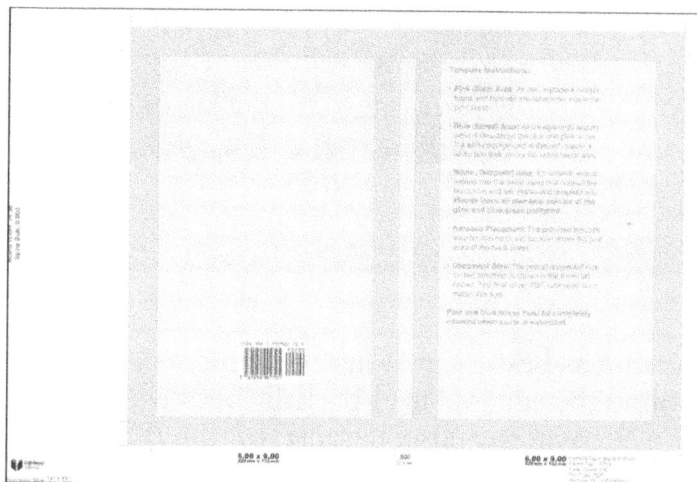

Notice that there is a wider blue border around the edge than for the paperback. Also, the blue space along the spine is much wider. Which is why even if you did your paperback in a 6 x 9 format, too, you'd still have a lot of moving pieces around to make this one work.

Also notice that the cover itself is positioned differently from the positioning of a paperback cover. Less of an issue when working in Affinity, but a big hassle for me when I used to work in GIMP.

First things first, go the Layers studio, select all, and group. (Ctrl + A, Ctrl + G)

Expand that group, take the first three layers and group them into their own subgroup. Move them above the larger group.

Click and drag the bar code that was created from that grouping to where you want it on the canvas. I put mine in the bottom right corner of the back cover.

Next, open your KDP print file or your IS paperback file. Select all but the group layer for the PDF template and the bar code, if applicable, copy (Ctrl + C), go back to your IS case laminate template, and paste (Ctrl + V).

Click and drag the group into place as best you can, but they're not going to fit because of the extra space the case laminate cover requires along the spine.

It's a starting point, though:

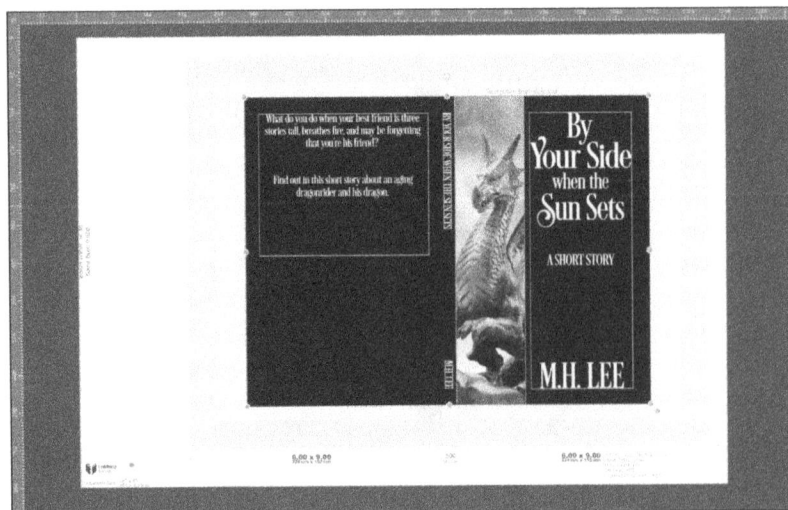

I've lined the cover up as best I can along the spine, but you can see there's a lot of extra space around the edges. This I partially because I'm moving from a 5.25 x 8 cover to a 6 x 9 cover but also because of the difference between a case laminate hard cover and a paperback cover.

Now that we have the layers generally where they need to be we can go through each one and make our necessary adjustments.

First up, the background layer. Click on it in the Layers studio to select just it and then go back to the canvas and drag from each edge to the edges of the blue perimeter for the cover.

You should see the green and red lines along the perimeter if you've matched it up with the cover template underneath.

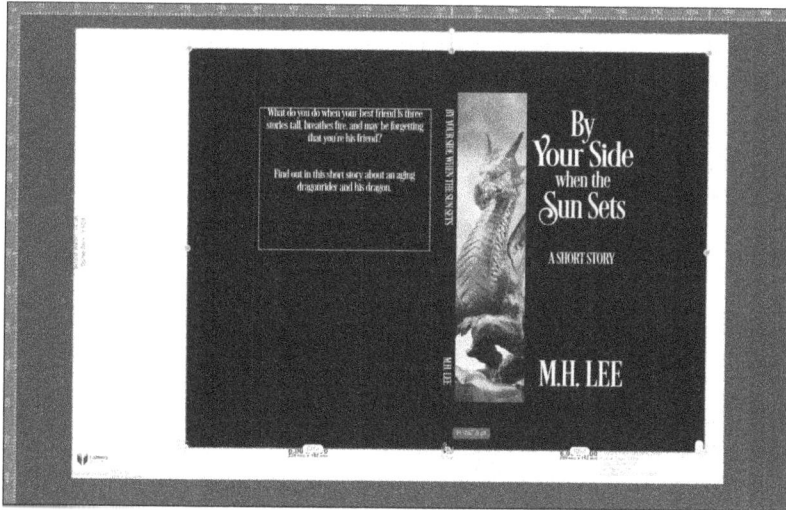

Hide that layer once you're done with it.

Now you can see how the other layers also need to be moved around:

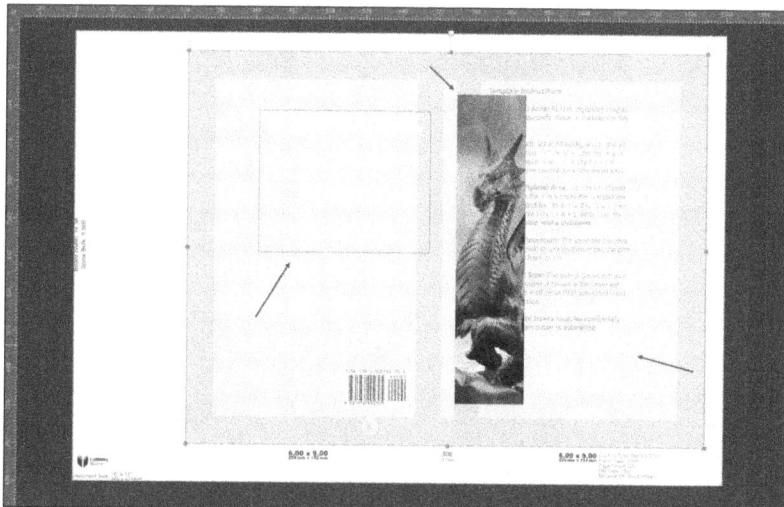

The spine text will need some adjustment, too, but since I placed the layers along the spine it's not off by near as much.

I'm going to start with the back cover copy. I click on that layer in the Layers studio to select it and then click on that text frame in the workspace and drag it over. One nice thing with this particular template is that Affinity will show when it's centered in the pink active area with a green line through the middle, so no guessing or having to move things around to see measurements.

Next up is the cover text and cover image. We can select both of those at once in the Layers studio and move them to the right until the cover image and text are in the pink space and not overlapping the blue area.

Also, I'm going to use the Transform studio here to resize everything so that I don't skew the text or the image.

I need to be careful here that the Lock Aspect Ratio option is turned on. I can confirm that it is when the little interlinking rings are visible on the right-hand side of the W and H value boxes.

Changing the width to 400 pt would give me the width to fill the space, but then the text is pretty close to the edge, so I went with 375. I had to then click and drag to position the image and text evenly within the pink work area:

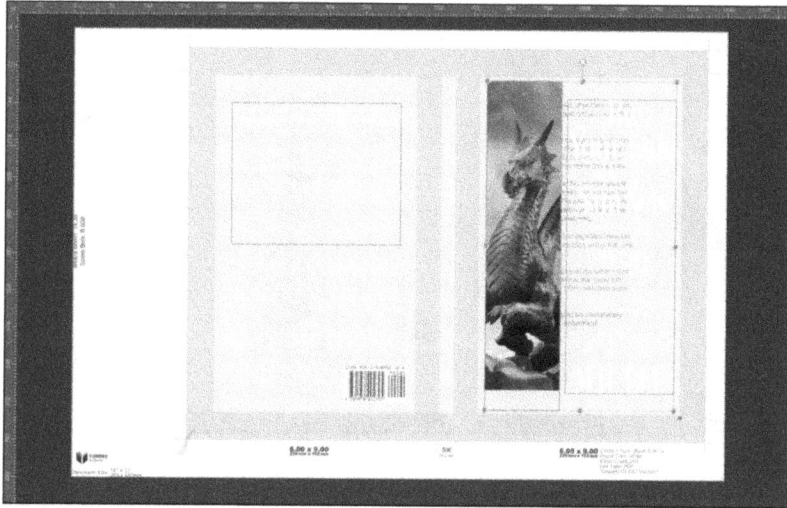

I now have a few changes to make that are particular to this cover.

See how the image and the author name aren't as far down towards the bottom of the pink space? I want to extend those down. I'm not going to extend the image into the blue areas, I'm okay having a black border on this one and letting it maybe be a little off. But I do at least want it to go as far down on the bottom side as it goes up on the top side.

So I click on the text frame layer and find that the frame is actually the right size. The issue is that the image needs to be moved down.

I expand the text frame layer, click on the image layer, and then click in my workspace and drag the image downward. I think it still works at its current size, so I'll leave it alone in that respect. If it didn't work I'd need to click on the corner and drag or use the Transform studio to resize it to fill the space better.

And if I did do that I'd also need to go to Document->Resource Manager to double-check that my Placed DPI value was still above 300 or I risk having a blurry or smudged printed image.

I also want the author name to drop down a bit as well.

I can click on that layer in the Layers studio and then click on the layer and use the down arrow to move the author name down more.

Be careful with covers that you choose the right layer. I'm inevitably trying to click on the author name from the spine when I need the one from the front cover.

I use the arrow key instead of clicking and dragging so I don't lose my alignment between the author name and the title.

That looks good now:

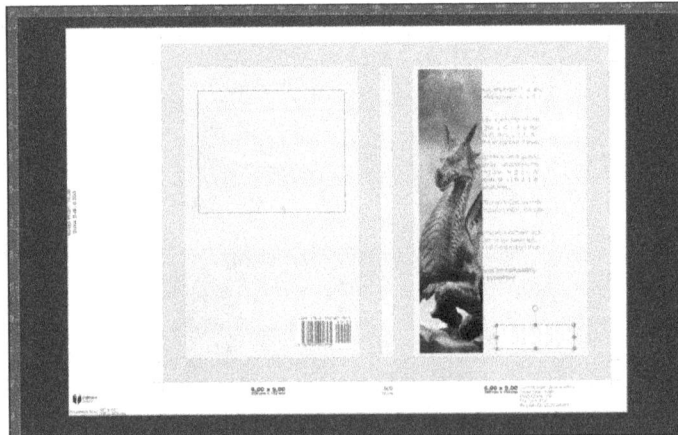

All that's left is to check on my spine text. It's easiest to do if you zoom in. And as we did before, I usually move the spine text pink space layer up to just below my title and author name layers while I'm working on this.

One other thing to note with case laminate covers is that they do sometimes allow you to use a larger font than you used on the equivalent paperback. It's your call whether you size that text up a bit or not. I'm not going to here.

Zoom back out. Turn on the rectangle layer. Drag the bar code layer above it. Drag the pink spine text layer below the rectangle layer. And you're done.

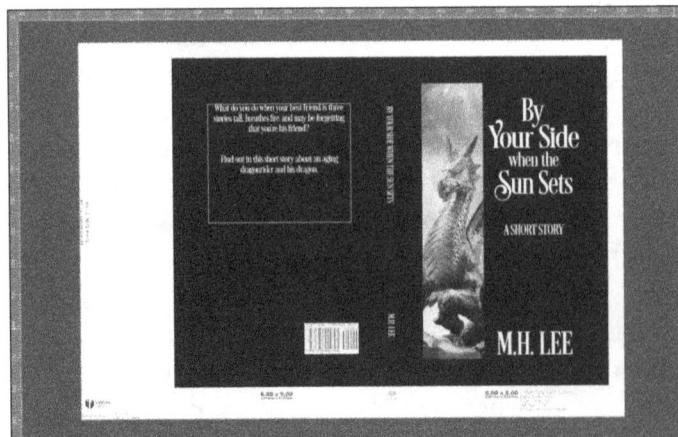

Because of the excess wraparound for a case laminate cover it can look odd in the template. The best time to really know what it will look like on the front cover at least is in the preview file you get from IngramSpark. (One could wish you saw that before you submit to them, but that's not how their process works. At least at that point you can just go and upload a new cover if needed without paying to do so again.)

And, done. Export as PDF. Same as the other IS cover, I use the PDF/X-1a:2003 setting.

CONCLUSION

Alright. That's it. We have now covered the basics of creating an ebook cover as well as print covers for IngramSpark and Amazon.

With the tools we covered here you should be able to create perfectly workable covers for most genres. And probably more attractive covers than I create.

The tools are what they are, what you make of them comes down to your design skills, practice, and patience.

Just like with writing, expect to get it wrong the first few times. And to not see that you got it wrong until later. Asking for a friend's opinion and getting silence tells you something. (As much as we'd like to wish it didn't.)

If you do get really serious about cover design, you're probably going to want to buy Affinity Photo and do a lot of your work there. That's where you need to go to work with Photoshop templates, for example. And where you can use layer masks to make text stand out on a busy background.

The good news is that most Photoshop videos and courses can be applied to Affinity Photo. You might have to look up what the tool is called in Affinity or where it's located, but for the most part I've been able to find Photoshop videos and take what I see there and almost immediately apply it in Affinity Photo.

I know that was true at least with the NeoStock videos on cover design where they do some pretty amazing stuff that leaves me in awe of the level of effort and amazing results. Those courses use Photoshop, but the concepts remain the same.

Now, is doing your own covers ideal? No, of course not.

In an ideal world we'd all be able to get immediate access to a top-level cover designer and have the money to burn to pay $500+ for an amazing cover for even the most basic of short stories.

But we don't live in an ideal world. And learning to do your own covers lets you (a) publish things you wouldn't otherwise, (b) pivot quickly, and (c) potentially earn more money.

I'll close with one final thought: Don't be afraid to try and fail. Very often in indie-world you are going to run into people who are very vocal about their judgements. According to them you can't self-edit, you can't make your own covers, you can't publish a novel until you've spent a decade honing your craft, etc. Basically, you're doing it wrong unless you're spending a fortune and an expert before you even begin.

And only if you're making seven figures a year can you possibly argue with them on these points. Of course, if you are making seven figures a year and doing any of that yourself then they'll just say you're an outlier and no one else could do that so they're still right.

But here's the deal.

I know too many authors who had beautiful packaging and failed.

Because what they needed was the type of editing most of us can neither find nor afford. Or they needed to learn about hitting the market. Everything about the book was fine, but the market they wrote for was a hundred people, half of whom don't buy self-published books.

And since they'd "done everything right" they gave up. If they could spend thousands for editing and covers and sell fifty copies then what was the point? So they walked away.

The beauty of doing this yourself is that you can do what my Wharton professor told us in our entrepreneurship class: "fail fast, fail cheap". Or, the corollary, succeed fast and cheap and then fix your mistakes on the fly. You're not locked into anything in this business.

Now, don't get me wrong. I'm not saying put out crap work. I'm saying get it to the point where it's good enough for people to try and then get them to try it without bankrupting yourself in the process. If you have something people like, they'll tell you with their money. They'll buy it. If you don't, they'll tell you with their silence. (Hopefully. Because that's certainly better than getting a bunch of bad reviews or nasty emails.)

Once you have a glimmer that what you've created has potential, then you can see about putting in all of that money.

And, yes, I realize that some will make the chicken and the egg argument here: Without good covers you can't get good sales. But as someone who has put books up with covers I've made myself, I can tell you that you will know when you've hit on something that people are interested in. And if that happens? The best thing to do…

Write more of it. As soon as you can.

You can rebrand later. First, get more product into the hands of the people who already found you and loved you.

Okay. Anyway. I digress and I'm probably preaching to the choir here if you read this far.

So let's close this out.

There is also a video course version of this book available on my Teachable store at https://ml-humphrey.teachable.com/. Use code MLH50 to get fifty percent off the course cost.

Also, if you hadn't already, you might want to check out *Affinity Publisher for Ad Creatives*, which walks you through how to use Affinity Publisher to create ad images for Amazon A+ Content, Facebook ads, Bookbub ads, and more.

Good luck with it. Feel free to reach out if you have questions. Even if I don't know the answer I'm usually pretty good at tracking them down.

APPENDIX A: AFFINITY PUBLISHER QUICK TAKES

BACKGROUND COLOR

ADD

See Rectangle Insert and then Color Apply Specific.

COLOR

APPLY SPECIFIC

To apply a specific color use the Color studio. Double-click on the filled circle or doughnut, whichever is on top, to open the Color Chooser dialogue box. Enter your specific values in the fields for RGB, HSL, CMYK, or the color's hex value next to the # sign. For bright yellow I use FFD500.

CHANGE

For text and fill color there will often be a rounded rectangle in the dynamic menu bar at top showing the current color. Click on that to see a dropdown menu of color choices. The Swatches tab is best for black, white, and shades of gray as well as recent colors used in the document. The Color tab is good for all other solid colors. The eyedropper on the Color tab can be used to choose a color from the canvas. Click on the color swatch you want or into the rectangle of shaded colors in the Color tab to apply. For the eyedropper, double-click on the color next to the eyedropper to apply.

ELEMENTS

CENTER

Layers studio. Select element or elements. Alignment dropdown in top menu. Align Center under Align Horizontally to center left to right or Align Middle under Align Vertically to center top to bottom.

DISTRIBUTE EVENLY

Place left-most and right-most or top-most and bottom-most elements at the outer edge of desired range. Select all elements in the Layers studio.

Alignment dropdown in top menu. Align Horizontally, Space Horizontally to distribute evenly left to right. Align Vertically, Space Vertically to distribute evenly top to bottom.

GROUP AND MOVE

Layers studio. Group layers. Move Tool. Left-click and drag.

GROUP AND RESIZE

Layers studio. Group layers. Click on grouped layers in workspace. Left-click and drag from blue circles around perimeter.

EXPORT

JPG

Go to File and then Export. Choose JPEG at the top of the dialogue box. Set Quality to around 85. Click on Export. Navigate to where you want to export the file. Edit the name if needed. Click on Save.

PDF

Go to File and then Export. Choose PDF. For KDP choose the PDF(press ready) option so that the file exports with bleed. For IngramSpark choose the PDF/X-1a:2003 option. Make sure DPI is 300 or more.

PNG

Go to File and then Export. Choose PNG at the top of the dialogue box. Click on Export. Navigate to where you want to export the file. Edit the name if needed. Click on Save.

FILE

NEW

Ctrl + N or go to File and then New in the top menu. Or you can choose New Document when you open Affinity.

OPEN

Ctrl + O or go to File and then Open. Navigate to the file, click on it, click on Open. For a file that was recently open you can go to File and then Open Recent and choose the file from the secondary dropdown menu.

SAVE

Ctrl + S or go to File and then Save in the top menu. To rename or save the file to a new location go to File and then Save As.

GUIDE LINES

ADD

Left-click and drag from the ruler around the workspace onto the canvas. Dragging from the top will add a horizontal line. Dragging from the left side will add a vertical line.

REMOVE

Left-click and drag the guideline off of the workspace. If you can't select the guideline, make sure that the Move Tool is selected first.

HEART

SHAPE INSERT

Rectangle Tool dropdown. Heart Tool. Left-click and drag on the canvas.

IMAGE

CONVERT TO BLACK AND WHITE

Select image layer in Layers studio. Go to Layer then New Adjustment and Black & White. Or click on the Layer Adjustments half-filled circle at the bottom of the Layers studio and choose Black & White from the dropdown menu there.

FLIP

Select the image layer. Go to Layer, then Transform, and then choose Flip Horizontal or Flip Vertical.

INSERT

Place Image Tool. Select image to insert. Open. Image may automatically insert. If not, click and drag in workspace until desired size.

INSERT IN PICTURE FRAME

Click on picture frame layer. Place Image Tool. Select image to insert. Open. Image will insert in frame.

LOCK ASPECT RATIO

In the Transform studio left-click on the two links with a small bar connecting them to the right side of the fields for the W and H values. If Lock Aspect Ratio is enabled there will be a line that extends from the links and connect them to the two fields. If it is not enabled there will just be the two links.

MOVE

Move Tool. Click in the center of the four arrows in the center of the image if in a picture frame. Or go to the image layer and click directly on the image. Hold left-click and drag to desired location.

REPLACE

Document top menu option. Resource Manager. Select image. Replace. Select new image. Open. Close resource manager.

RESIZE

Move Tool. Click on image layer or directly on image if not in a picture frame. Option A: Transform studio. Lock Aspect Ratio. Change height or width value. Option B: Click on blue circle in corner and drag at an angle to resize proportionately. Or click on blue circle along any edge to change height or width only. This will skew most images.

RESIZE IN PICTURE FRAME

If you are clicked into the picture frame layer there will be a slider below the frame. You can move the slider to the right or left to resize the image in the picture frame.

ROTATE

Select the image layer. Go to Layer, Transform, Rotate Right or Rotate Left. Or go to the Transform studio and enter a value for R. Or left-click on the white filled circle outside the perimeter of the image and hold that left-click as you drag to the right or the left.

SEPIA

Apply Black & White layer adjustment to the image layer. Then go to Layer and Layer Effects or click on the Layer Effects option at the bottom of the Layers studio. Check the box for Color Overlay. Click on the text for Color Overlay. Change Opacity to approximately 50%. Change the color to a darker golden-toned brown color.

LAYER

DELETE

Right-click on the layer in the Layers studio and select Delete from the dropdown menu or click on the layer and use the Delete key.

DUPLICATE

Right-click on the layer in the Layers studio and select Duplicate from the dropdown menu.

GROUP

Select the layers you want to group using the Ctrl key (for layers that are not adjacent) or the Shift key (for layers that are). Left-click on each layer and hold down Shift or Ctrl as you select the rest. Then use Ctrl + G to group the layers or right-click and select Group from the dropdown menu.

HIDE

Uncheck the box next to the layer name in the Layers studio.

MOVE

Left-click and drag a layer up or down to its desired position. The blue shading will show where the layer will go. You can also use the gray and yellow box images in the top menu to move a layer all the way to the top, all the way to the bottom, or up or down one space.

TRANSPARENCY

To change the transparency of a layer, select it in the Layers studio, click on the dropdown for Opacity at the top of the studio, and then adjust the slider to the desired degree of transparency.

UNGROUP

Right-click on the grouped layers in the Layers studio and choose Ungroup from the dropdown menu. Or use Ctrl + Shift + G.

UNHIDE

Check the box next to the layer name in the Layers studio.

NEW DOCUMENT PRESET

ADD

File->Open to start a new document. Make changes in the New Document dialogue box to create a new layout. Click on the + sign next to Custom at the top of the layout settings.

CHOOSE

In the New Document dialogue box click on the preset and then click on Create. Some presets will be under different headings such as Print, Press Ready, etc. and you will need to click on that heading first.

RENAME

Right-click on the thumbnail for the preset. Choose Rename Preset. Type new name. OK.

PICTURE FRAME

BORDER

Select the picture frame layer in the Layers studio. Make sure the Move Tool is selected. To add a border, in the dynamic menu at the top, click on the white line with a red slash through it to the right of Stroke and change the Width value to the desired width. Click on the colored field next to Stroke to change the color of the line. To remove a border, click on the solid line to the right of Stroke in the dynamic menu and then click on the circle with a red slash through the middle next to Style in the dropdown menu.

INSERT

Picture Frame Rectangle Tool. Click and drag to place picture frame on canvas.

MOVE

Select the picture frame layer in the Layers studio. If the Move Tool is selected, left-click anywhere on the frame in the workspace and drag. If the Text Tool is selected, left-click on the perimeter of the frame and drag. Or use the Transform studio to provide a specific X or Y value.

RESIZE

Select the picture frame layer in the Layers studio. Left-click and drag from any of the blue circles around the perimeter of the frame.

RESIZE FRAME AND IMAGE SIMULTANEOUSLY

Select the picture frame layer in the Layers studio. Left-click and drag from the blue circle outside of the perimeter of the frame in the bottom right corner.

RECTANGLE

ANGLE

Select the layer for the rectangle in the Layers studio. Go to the Transform studio and change the S value.

INSERT

Rectangle Tool. Left-click and drag on the canvas.

SELECT ALL

SELECT ALL

Ctrl + A.

SNAPPING

ENABLE

Go to the horseshoe shaped magnet image in the top center of the top menu. Click on the dropdown arrow. Check the box next to Enable Snapping.

STAR

SHAPE INSERT

Rectangle Tool dropdown. Star Tool. Left-click and drag on the canvas.

TEXT INSERT

Artistic Text Tool. Glyph Browser. Wingdings font. Double-click on star shape.

STUDIO

ANCHOR

Left-click on studio and drag to the left or right-hand side of the workspace until you see a blue outline appear and then release. To move within a series of tabs, simply left-click and drag.

CLOSE

Go to View and then Studio and select the name of the studio you want to close. Or, left-click on the studio, drag it away from the workspace so that it is a standalone dialogue box, and click on the top right corner to close it.

MOVE

Left-click on studio dialogue box or tab and drag to move to desired location.

OPEN

Go to View and then Studio and select the studio you want.

STUDIO PRESET

ADD NEW

Arrange studios as desired. Go to View in top menu. Then Studio Presets. Add Preset. Type name. OK.

APPLY

Option 1: Go to View in top menu and then Studio Presets and select desired preset. Option 2: Ctrl + Shift + [Number] for the desired preset.

DELETE

Go to View in top menu. Then Studio Presets and Manage Studio Presets. Select preset name. Delete. Close.

RENAME

Go to View in top menu. Then Studio Presets and Manage Studio Presets. Select preset name. Rename. Type in new name. OK. Close.

RESET

To reset to the original studio preset go to View and then Studio and Reset Studio.

SAVE CHANGES

Make desired changes to studio preset arrangement. Go to View in top menu. Then Studio Presets. Add Preset. Type in exact same name as before. OK. Agree to overwrite old preset when prompted.

TEXT

ADD

To add text directly onto your canvas, select the Artistic Text Tool, and then click on the canvas and type. You may need to left-click on the canvas and drag to form an A before you can type.

ADD SPECIAL SYMBOLS OR CHARACTERS

Artistic Text Tool. Click into workspace where desired. Go to the Glyph Browser. Find desired symbol or character. Double-click on symbol or character to insert.

ALIGNMENT (LEFT TO RIGHT)

Artistic Text Tool. Click on the text layer. Go to the menu choices in the dynamic menu above the workspace. There are four images with lines. Align Left, Align Center, Align Right, or use the dropdown menu for Justify Left, Justify Center, Justify Right, Justify All, Align Towards Spine, Align Away From Spine.

ALIGNMENT (TOP TO BOTTOM)

Artistic Text Tool. Click on the text layer. Go to the menu choices in the dynamic menu above the workspace. Use the dropdown menu for Top Align, Center Vertically, Bottom Align, or Justify Vertically.

ALL CAPS OR SMALL CAPS

Artistic Text Tool. Select the text to be formatted. Go to Character studio. Typography section. Click on the two capital Ts (TT) to apply all caps. Click on the capital T with a lowercase T (Tt) to apply small caps.

FONT

Artistic Text Tool. Select text. Dynamic menu at top, left-hand side. Font dropdown. Choose font. Or select text and go to Character studio font dropdown at top.

LINE SPACING (LEADING)

Artistic Text Tool. Select paragraph. Paragraph studio. Spacing section. Change value in Leading dropdown. Default is usually a good place to start. With design work it's often better to just have each line of text as its own layer so you can manually adjust the spacing between elements.

ROTATE

Select the layer with the text you want to rotate and then change the R value in the Transform studio. You can also left-click and drag the white circle outside the edge of the text layer from the canvas itself.

SIZE

Artistic Text Tool. Select text. Dynamic menu at top, left-hand side. Font size dropdown. Choose size or type in size. Or select text and go to Character studio font size dropdown at top.

WEIGHT

Artistic Text Tool. Select text. Dynamic menu at top, left-hand side. Font weight dropdown. (Will usually default to Regular.) Choose from available weights for that font. Or select text and go to Character studio font weight dropdown at top.

TEXT FRAME

ALIGN OR POSITION

Frame Text Tool or Move Tool. Left-click on text frame and hold as you drag. Look for red and green alignment lines to center or align to other elements in workspace. (Turn on Snapping if there are no red or green lines.) Use Alignment dropdown in top menu to align to workspace, not the dynamic menu bar that applies to actual text.

INSERT

Frame Text Tool on left-hand side. Click and drag in workspace.

RESIZE

Click on text frame layer. Left-click and drag on one of the blue circles around the perimeter of the text. Click and drag at an angle from the corner to keep scaling proportionate.

UNDO

Ctrl + Z. Or you can open the History studio and rewind using the slider or by clicking back onto a prior step.

INDEX

ABOUT THE AUTHOR

M.L. Humphrey is a self-published author with both fiction and non-fiction titles published under a variety of pen names. When she gets stuck on her next fiction project she foolishly decides to write books that only ten people are going to buy, although she does usually learn something interesting in the process so it's worth it in the end.

You can reach her at:

mlhumphreywriter@gmail.com

or at

www.mlhumphrey.com

www.ingramcontent.com/pod-product-compliance
Lightning Source LLC
Chambersburg PA
CBHW080626030426
42336CB00018B/3089

* 9 7 8 1 6 3 7 4 4 0 2 9 2 *